# First Fruits

## About the authors

**Adrian Mann** is on the Board of the Anglican Stewardship Association and is author of *No Small Change*, also published by the Canterbury Press. He is a reader in the Diocese of St Edmundsbury and Ipswich.

**Robin Stevens** is National Stewardship Officer of the Church of England and also serves as a reader in the Diocese of Chelmsford.

**John Willmington** is a parish priest in London and on the Board of the Anglican Stewardship Association.

# First Fruits

*A worship anthology on generosity and giving*

*Compiled by*

Adrian Mann, Robin Stevens and
John Willmington

CANTERBURY
PRESS
Norwich

Copyright © in this compilation the Anglican Stewardship
Association 2001

First published in 2001 by The Canterbury Press Norwich
(a publishing imprint of Hymns Ancient & Modern Limited
a registered charity)
St Mary's Works, St Mary's Plain
Norwich, Norfolk, NR3 3BH

British Library Cataloguing in Publication Data

A catalogue record of this book is available
from the British Library

ISBN 1-85311-392-1

Typeset by Rowland Phototypesetting Ltd,
Bury St Edmunds, Suffolk
Printed in Great Britain by
Biddles Ltd, Guildford and King's Lynn

# The General Thanksgiving

Almighty God, Father of all mercies,
we your unworthy servants
give you most humble and hearty thanks
for all your goodness and loving kindness.
We bless you for our creation, preservation,
and all the blessings of this life;
but above all for your immeasurable love
in the redemption of the world
by our Lord Jesus Christ,
for the means of grace and for the hope of glory.
And give us, we pray,
such a sense of all your mercies
that our hearts may be unfeignedly thankful,
and that we show forth your praise,
not only with our lips but in our lives,
by giving up ourselves to your service,
and by walking before you
in holiness and righteousness, all our days;
through Jesus Christ our Lord,
to whom, with you and the Holy Spirit,
be honour and glory,
for ever and ever. Amen.

# Contents

# Introduction

## Money

### Jesus and Money

When we read New Testament accounts of Jesus with people, he often speaks about money and wealth. Attitudes to money and wealth are signs and symptoms of where people are. Actions about money and wealth are agents for change in the whole person.

'Where your treasure is, there will your heart be also' (Matthew 6:21). Jesus is discerning, penetrating and direct about this. It is here, in how we handle our money, that much of human nature is revealed. In our day social and global change has done nothing to diminish this simple, profound truth.

Our personal economic circumstances are part and parcel of who we are. To have financial resources enables us to participate and to cope with incessant change; to lack them cuts us off from much that we want to do or have or see or be.

Wealth is powerful: this is the unaltering message. It is powerful in society and in human relationships. It is powerful in our hearts and minds, in our spirits. Money can measure all sorts of things about us, about our way of life and how we practise our faith. More than that, it can play upon our souls in complex ways.

### Worship and Money

All this needs to find its place in our worship. Worship should grant each of us a place to encounter the living God: to approach and to heed, to adore and to honour. Little of this can come to pass without an honest attempt on our part to bring our real selves before the real God. This must include our thoughts and feelings and actions about money.

It is one thing to say this, but quite another to do it, which is why we need the objectivity of worship, the structure and ritual of worship, the companionship in worship of a community. These are vehicles of grace, which carry us and help us face the challenges that need to be there.

## The Church and Money

The Church has always found money a difficult subject. It is a human institution, so this should not be so surprising in the light of what Jesus has to say about human beings and money. The Church needs money to do its work, but it also has to say difficult and prophetic things to us about wealth. It is not easy to hold both these truths at once.

Many Christians have felt talk of money to be unspiritual and somehow out of place in the Church. This spiritualizing approach has left a dangerous vacuum. All too often our talk about money is then driven by need: the need to maintain institutional structures, the need to do important work.

Of course, these can be worthy needs, but they cannot be as important as Jesus' insights about the part money plays in our lives. The nagging questions remain. Why (in the light of Jesus' quite different practice) does the Church only talk about money when it wants some? Why do we fall short in terms of giving and generosity?

## The Christian and Money

But *we* are the Church after all, the worshipping community, the community with universal claims. We cannot simply blame the Church for these failures, for they are our failures, too. They serve our purposes. They protect us from the challenge of a real encounter with what our Christian faith may really be saying to us about money.

If we are asked to consider the need of the Church to receive financial contributions from us, that leaves us feeling quite comfortable, nicely in control and not very challenged. We are the donors, the Church is the supplicant, and that gives us the upper hand.

However, if we are asked to reflect upon our own economic relationships in the light of God's call to justice and to respond in terms of generosity and sacrifice, that stretches us. Now we are part of the body of Christ, challenged to follow the Christian way of life, and no one has the upper hand except our forgiving Lord. We are called to offer up whatever control of our own life money has given us. We are called to worship.


## Moving towards God

As we worship we offer what we are in all its inadequacy, what we have in all its poverty, what we do in all its wrongfulness. We do this in faith and hope that it will by grace be transformed into something for God, even something of God. This is the movement we long for and seek in worship, above all in the Eucharist. It sounds and is presumptuous, but we dare to think this way because of what Christ has done for us. He has shared our humanity and offered us his divinity.

This same movement has dictated the shape of this book of material for worship. What is here can be used in all sorts of circumstances by all sorts of people, but its form follows the pattern of the Eucharist, the great thanksgiving of the Church.

Into this pattern we have tried to bring something of the reality of our human attitudes to money and wealth, so that it can in turn be used as an offering of human reality to God. This combination of form and content expresses something essential about our human condition. That is why there is an urgency and a necessity about what is being attempted.

So here is the opportunity to connect life and worship by addressing the subject of money *within* worship. Our use of money is a tangible expression of so many of our relationships – with family, friends and loved ones; with those we work with or for; with those we buy from or sell to; with those we give to or take from. It speaks of our attitudes to others and to the whole of creation.

Not least, the use of money expresses our relationship with the poor: bringing Lazarus to our gate wherever he or we may be. Economic connections *are* relationships. However difficult we may find it, surely this must be admitted to our worship, to our reaching out to God. We *do* find it difficult and so we are thankful that Christianity has a place for those who fail, and that we can bring this failure with us into the healing arena of worship.

Economic connections are relationships that matter to God. But sadly all this finds little place in our formal liturgies, even after many years of liturgical renewal. There is a huge gap in published material, which this book is in a small way trying to fill. This gap is a sign of an underlying gap between Christian worship and the reality of Christian lives.

Christians are not immune from the inescapable power of money in every area of life. The failure of the churches to bridge this gap has contributed to their inexorable shift to the margins of relevance. There is a whole language we are failing to speak. Here is an attempt to bring that language into our worship.

# How to Use this Book and Disk

## Using the Book

This book tries to provide ways to bring money, and particularly generosity and the giving of money, into worship. It is intended both for regular and occasional use, for special services and for adding into day-by-day and week-by-week worship as appropriate. We encourage you to consider that there is a continual need to bring before God a difficult and much misunderstood topic.

We have not tried to provide a rigid blueprint, but rather a variety of material in a variety of styles. It can be used flexibly and should be used creatively. It is organized in a Eucharistic shape – we hope that this will make it easy for people to find their way about it – but this is not intended to dictate *how* it should be used. The final section 'Service Outlines' gives ideas for particular events, but there is no need to follow this rigidly if circumstances suggest otherwise.

The use of silence or of movement, or of communal action – particularly at the offertory – can highlight in fresh ways the relevance of what is happening. It is not our intention to prescribe how this should be done, for it is important for people to make the material their own, to relate it to their own insights by their own imaginations, to make it part of their own worshipping lives. Particular ideas are offered in boxes in the relevant sections of the book.

## Music, Hymns and Songs

- The book contains a varied collection of work by some of our most talented hymn- and songwriters.
- For ease of use we have concentrated on providing new words for known tunes.
- There is also some completely new material providing stylistic variety.

## Preaching and Teaching

- Remember that there is a need for continuing teaching on the subject of money and giving: it is a much misunderstood subject.
- Adopt a tone of thanksgiving to God: this should always be the basis for our thoughts and prayers about money.
- Never apologize for addressing this important topic: this will undermine everything else you say.
- Avoid special pleading for the Church's needs. There are many needs in the world. It is far better to give positive encouragement towards a joyful response to God's own abundant giving.
- This is about putting our faith into action, as the Gospel stories about people and money clearly tell us. Fear of this topic can be addressed by honest attempts to practise what you preach!

## Communal Action

- What we do with our money should be an acted parable in harmony with our worship.
- Generous corporate giving is sign of a healthy Church community.
- Christian giving based on thanksgiving is life-enhancing and attractive to others. It is a positive advertisement for the Church.
- Fundraising from others for things we should be providing can send out a negative message: it shows a community that needs to receive, rather than one that needs to give.
- Remember the distinction: 'Stewardship is asking ourselves, fundraising is asking others.'

- Fundraising *can* be appropriate for social action and the relief of poverty, enabling the Church community to lead and encourage others in the way of giving.

## Pastoral Care

- Pastoral care, money and worship are closely linked: they are all about people.
- Unease about the subject of money may make us want to separate these spheres: it is unwise, unrealistic and counterproductive to do so.

## Thoughts of Encouragement

- There is a strong base to build on: altruism is intrinsic to the gospel, and research shows that Christians give more than others.
- This is something to proclaim, to celebrate, and for which to give thanks: taking us into fuller response.
- Differences between congregations and the well-documented greater generosity of poorer church communities show there is still a long way to go.
- Here is the chance to make a real change and to live out a faith which is demonstrably relevant to the realities of life today.

# Using the Disk

The accompanying disk contains the text of the worship material in both Microsoft Word and Rich Text Format (RTF). The Word version will be suitable for those using Microsoft packages but it can be used by many other up to date word processors. The RTF format text will be suitable for those who cannot make use of Word.

There are two main directories (folders) on the disk, one for each format. In each directory, the text of the material is given in sub-directories – one for each chapter. To copy the material that you wish to use for a particular service, you should go into your word processor and then search for the material on the disk by going to the appropriate main directory for your system and then the sub-directory for the chapter that you want to use. Scroll down until you reach the material you want, highlight the material and then copy it. Go back to the document of the service that you are preparing and place the cursor at the point at which you want to insert the material. Paste the text in at that point. You may need to reformat the text to suit the particular document that you are creating.

For example, in order to place a hymn in a service sheet, open the disk from your word processor. If it supports Word files, select the Word folder and then select chapter 14 for hymns and songs. Scroll through the hymns until you find the one you want. Highlight the hymn by dragging the cursor across it with the left mouse button pressed. Press the right mouse button and select copy. Now go back to your service sheet and paste the hymn into its place in the service sheet.

## Christian Copyright Licensing

Please note the following information about copying hymns and songs where the copyright is held by Stainer and Bell Ltd, Kevin Mayhew Ltd, Josef Weinberger Ltd, or Jubilate Hymns. These items are individually identified in the book.

Copies may be made for local church use if you hold a current Church Copying Licence and include the work on your return to Christian Copyright Licensing (Europe) Ltd. Alternatively, you need to write to the copyright holder for permission. The relevant addresses can be found in 'Acknowledgements and Sources' on p. 125.

# I

# Sentences

All shall give as they are able, according to the blessings of the Lord your God that he has given you.

*Deuteronomy 16:17*

I bring the first of the fruit of the ground that you, O Lord, have given me.

*Deuteronomy 26:10a*

My vows to you I must perform, O God; I will render thank-offerings to you. For you have delivered my soul from death, and my feet from falling, so that I may walk before God in the light of life.

*Psalms 56:12–13*

Honour the Lord with your substance and with the first fruits of all your produce.

*Proverbs 3:9*

Do not store up for yourselves treasures on earth, where moth and rust consume and where thieves break in and steal; but store up for yourselves treasures in heaven, where neither moth nor rust consumes and where thieves do not break in and steal. For where your treasure is, there your heart will be also.

*Matthew 6:19–21*

Not everyone who says to me, 'Lord, Lord', will enter the kingdom of heaven, but only one who does the will of my Father in heaven.

*Matthew 7:21*

Give, and it will be given to you. A good measure, pressed down, shaken together, running over, will be put into your lap; for the measure you give will be the measure you get back.

*Luke 6:38*

Jesus said to them, 'Take care! Be on your guard against all kinds of greed; for one's life does not consist in the abundance of possessions.'

*Luke 12:15*

Remembering the words of the Lord Jesus, for he himself said, 'It is more blessed to give than to receive.'

*Acts 20:35b*

If the part of the dough offered as first fruits is holy, then the whole batch is holy; and if the root is holy, then the branches also are holy.

*Romans 11:16*

I appeal to you therefore, brothers and sisters, by the mercies of God, to present your bodies as a living sacrifice, holy and acceptable to God, which is your spiritual worship.

*Romans 12:1*

On the first day of every week, each one of you should set aside a sum of money in proportion to what has been earned.

*1 Corinthians 16:2a*

Now as you excel in everything – in faith, in speech, in knowledge, in utmost eagerness, and in your love for us – so we want you to excel also in this generous undertaking.

*2 Corinthians 8:7*

You know the grace of our Lord Jesus Christ, that though he was rich, yet for your sakes he became poor, so that by his poverty you might become rich.

*2 Corinthians 8:9*

For if the eagerness is there, the gift is acceptable according to what one has – not according to what one does not have.

*2 Corinthians 8:12*

The one who sows sparingly will also reap sparingly, and the one who sows bountifully will also reap bountifully. Each of you must give as you have made up your mind, not reluctantly or under compulsion, for God loves a cheerful giver.

*2 Corinthians 9:6–7*

God is able to provide you with every blessing in abundance, so that by always having enough of everything, you may share abundantly in every good work.

*2 Corinthians 9:8*

There is great gain in godliness combined with contentment; for we brought nothing into the world, so that we can take nothing out of it.

*1 Timothy 6:6–7*

As for those who in the present age are rich, command them to set their hope on God who richly provides us with everything for our enjoyment. They are to be ready to share, thus storing up for themselves the treasure of a good foundation for the future.

*1 Timothy 6:17–19*

Keep your lives free from the love of money, and be content with what you have; because God has said, 'I will never leave you or forsake you.'

*Hebrews 13:5*

Do not neglect to do good and to share what you have, for such sacrifices are pleasing to God.

*Hebrews 13:16*

How does God's love abide in anyone who has the world's goods and sees a brother or sister in need and yet refuses to help?

*1 John 3:17*

# Penitence

When we have sown sparingly;
Lord, have mercy.
**Lord, have mercy.**

When we have given reluctantly;
Christ, have mercy.
**Christ, have mercy.**

That we may know the joy of cheerful giving;
Lord, have mercy.
**Lord, have mercy.**

*Stewardship Network Resource Book (adapted)*

Father in creation, you are generous towards us;
When we are tight-fisted in return;
Lord, have mercy.
**Lord, have mercy.**

Jesus, you call us to turn to you;
When we are deaf to your call;
Christ, have mercy.
**Christ, have mercy.**

Holy Spirit, you show us the gift of charity;
When we fail to respond;
Lord, have mercy.
**Lord, have mercy.**

*Stewardship Network Resource Book (adapted)*

Lord, when we have failed to recognize your presence;
Lord, have mercy.
**Lord, have mercy.**

Lord, when we have failed to recognize the needs of others;
Christ, have mercy.
**Christ, have mercy.**

Lord, when we have not responded generously to the call of the
   gospel;
Lord, have mercy.
**Lord, have mercy.**

*Stewardship Network Resource Book (adapted)*

Lord, you are the fullness of grace and truth.
Lord, have mercy.
**Lord, have mercy.**

You made yourself poor, that we might become rich.
Christ, have mercy.
**Christ, have mercy.**

You came to fashion us into your holy people.
Lord, have mercy.
**Lord, have mercy.**

*Libreria Editrice Vaticana*
*00120 Città del Vaticano*

Defender of the poor;
Lord, have mercy.
**Lord, have mercy.**

Refuge of the powerless;
Christ, have mercy.
**Christ, have mercy.**

Hope of sinners;
Lord, have mercy.
**Lord, have mercy.**

*Libreria Editrice Vaticana*
*00120 Città del Vaticano*

# 3

# Collects and Prayers

Almighty God our heavenly Father,
you declare your glory and show forth your handiwork
in the heavens and in the earth:
deliver us in our various occupations
from the service of self alone,
that we may do the work you give us to do
in truth and beauty and for the common good;
for the sake of him who came among us as one who serves,
your Son Jesus Christ our Lord.

*Church of the Province of the West Indies*

Christ Jesus,
as you had compassion on the starving multitudes,
let that mind be in us also which was in you,
that we may have the will and the wisdom
   to work until all be fed,
to your glory and through your grace and love.

*© Michael Counsell*
*Prayers for Sundays*
*(HarperCollins Publishers Ltd 1994)*

Eternal God,
open our eyes to see your hand at work
in the splendour of creation
   and in the beauty of human life.
Help us to cherish the gifts that surround us,

to share our blessings with our sisters and brothers,
and to experience the joy of life in your presence;
through Jesus Christ our Lord.

Prayer Book for Australia

Father God, you sent your Son Jesus to give up
everything for us:
may the gifts we bring (today),
whether great or small,
be the very best that we can offer
and a sign of our grateful love;
through Jesus Christ our Lord.

© Jenny Dann<br>
Maybe linked with the song 'What will you give . . .'

Father, in the mystery of your Son, poor and crucified,
you have chosen to enrich us with every good gift:
grant that we may fear neither poverty nor the cross,
but rejoice to bring our brothers and sisters
the good news of life restored and renewed;
through Jesus Christ our Lord.

Libreria Editrice Vaticana<br>
00120 Città del Vaticano

Father of all,
you loved the world so much that you gave your only Son,
so that all who believe in him
should have eternal and abundant life:
grant us grace to accept all your gifts and to use them
   for the good of others,
   for the care of your world
and to proclaim the values of your kingdom;
through Jesus Christ our Lord.

© Anglican Stewardship Association

Generous God,
we know that all that we have is yours:
save us from the delusion
of believing it is ours;
save us from our possessiveness,
that your grace may abound
in all things at all times;
through Jesus Christ our Saviour.

*Lambeth Prayers (ACC/SPCK 1998)*

Generous God,
whose hand is open
to fill all things living with plenteousness:
make us ever thankful for your goodness,
and grant that we, remembering the account
    that we must one day give,
may be faithful stewards of your bounty;
through Jesus Christ our Lord.

*Prayer Book for Australia*

God of those who have nothing,
your Son on earth knew trouble and pain,
betrayal and desertion, dishonour and death:
may we rejoice in you,
in whom we possess everything
and are rich beyond measure;
through Jesus Christ our Lord.

*Lambeth Prayers (ACC/SPCK 1998)*

God our Father,
you scrutinize our thoughts and motives,
and nothing you have created can hide itself from you:
penetrate our hearts with the sword of your word,

that, in the light of your wisdom,
we may be able to value rightly the things of time and eternity,
and become poor and free for the sake of your kingdom;
through Jesus Christ our Lord.

*Libreria Editrice Vaticana*
*00120 Città del Vaticano*


God, you have made our world
and seen that it is good:
grant to us, created to complete your work,
the bright, delightful vision
that makes us care for what we do.

You made us, Lord, and we are yours:
grant that we may so use your gifts
that all your creatures may enjoy the harmony you planned.

*A New Zealand Prayer Book (adapted)*
*Anglican Church in Aotearoa, New Zealand and Polynesia*


Heavenly Father, source of all life,
we thank you for the many ways
in which you have blessed and enriched our lives:
keep us from possessiveness and greed,
and lead us into the greater joy
of sharing your gifts with others.
Through Jesus Christ, in whom is perfect peace.

© *Jenny Dann*
*May be linked with the hymn 'All you have given . . .'*


Heavenly Father,
you taught us by your Son Jesus Christ
    that all our possessions come from you:
help us to be faithful stewards of our time,
    our talents and our wealth,

and to consecrate gladly to your service
　　a due proportion for all that you have given us.
Take us and make us your own;
for Jesus Christ's sake.

　　　　　　　　　　　　　　　*© Central Board of Finance*

Hidden God,
whose wisdom compels our love
　　and unsettles all our values:
fill us with desire to search for her truth,
that, becoming fools for her sake,
we may transform the world,
through Jesus Christ,
　　your word and wisdom made flesh,
to whom be glory for ever.

　　　　　　　　　　　　　　　*Prayer Book for Australia*

Living Christ,
you have known insecurity and poverty:
free us from the need to seek
the security of easy wealth.
Give us generous hearts,
that we may know the richness of your grace.
For your holy name's sake.

　　　　　　　*Lambeth Prayers (adapted) (ACC/SPCK, 1998)*

Lord Jesus,
grant that as through your saving grace
we have become rich in many ways,
so may we have joy in sharing our riches,
within your Church
for the sake of your kingdom.

　　　　　　　　　　　　　　　*© Central Board of Finance*

Lord of all,
in a world marked by pain and suffering,
   yet saved by your intensity of giving,
make us thankful for our good fortune,
protect us from hardness of heart
   and teach us to respond with gratitude and generosity
   to you and to others;
through Jesus Christ our Saviour.

*© Anglican Stewardship Association*

Loving God,
you are generous and forgiving:
grant that we, living in comfort and security,
may accept your abundant love with gratitude and humility;
heal our guilt, dissolve our greed,
and send us out to meet the world and our neighbours
with thankful hearts and generous spirits.
Through Jesus Christ our Lord.

*© Anglican Stewardship Association*

O God, the fount of wisdom,
you have revealed to us in Christ
   the hidden treasure and the pearl of great price:
grant us your Spirit's gift of discernment,
that, in the midst of the things of this world,
we may learn to value the priceless worth of your kingdom,
and be ready to renounce all else
   for the sake of the precious gift you offer;
through Jesus Christ our Lord.

*Prayer Book for Australia*

O God,
you are rich in love for your people:
show us the treasure that endures
and, when we are tempted by greed,

call us back into your service
and make us worthy to be
    entrusted with the wealth that never fails;
through Jesus Christ our Lord.

*Prayer Book for Australia*

O God,
your Son has taught us
that those who give a cup of water in his name
    will not lose their reward:
open our eyes to see those who are in need,
and teach us to set no store by riches and earthly rewards,
so that, in surrendering ourselves to serve you
    in your children,
we may labour for the treasure that endures;
through Jesus Christ our Lord.

*Prayer Book for Australia*

O Lord Jesus Christ
by your incarnation you sanctified material things
    to be the means of your grace:
grant us a right attitude to money,
and a generous heart in the use of the
    wealth committed to us,
that by our stewardship we may glorify you,
with the Father and the Holy Spirit,
one God, now and for ever.

© *Central Board of Finance*

O merciful Creator,
your hand is open wide to satisfy the needs of every living creature:
make us always thankful for your loving providence;
and grant that we,
remembering the account that we must one day give,
may be faithful stewards of your good gifts;
through Jesus Christ our Lord.

*Church of the Province of the West Indies*

You are so generous, Lord,
    in your daily creative dealings with us.
You have formed an atmosphere, oceans and soil
    in which life can multiply,
and pour your sunshine and rain abundantly upon us.
As you have been so bountiful and open-hearted to us,
    make us equally generous in sharing what
    you have lent to us with those in need.
We offer our lives to you, as Jesus gave his life for us.

© *Michael Counsell*
*Prayers for Sundays*
*(HarperCollins Publishers Ltd 1994)*

# 4

# Praise

| | |
|---|---|
| Minister | Glory to the Father |
| **People** | **Glory to the Son** |
| | Glory to the Spirit |
| | **For ever Three in One** |

Be glorified at home
**Be glorified in church**
Be glorified in our work
**Be glorified in our play**
Be glorified in our land
**Be glorified in our neighbours**
Be glorified in earth
**Be glorified in heaven**

Glory to the Father
**Glory to the Son**
Glory to the Spirit
**For ever Three in One**

Hallelujah
**Amen**

*Anglican Church of Kenya (adapted)*
*Publishing House – Uzima Press*

## Psalm 33

*R:*  May your love be upon us, O Lord,
       As we have put our trust in you.

For the word of the Lord is right,
And all his works are sure.
He loves righteousness and justice;
The loving-kindness of the Lord fills the whole earth. *R.*

Behold, the eye of the Lord is upon those who fear him,
On those who wait upon his love,
To pluck their lives from death,
And to feed them in time of famine. *R.*

Our soul waits for the Lord;
He is our help and our shield.
Let your loving-kindness, O Lord, be upon us,
As we have put our trust in you. *R.*

© *Society of St Francis 1992*
*Celebrating Common Prayer (Mowbray)*

## Psalm 127

*R:*  May the Lord build us a house,
       And watch over the city.

Unless the Lord builds the house,
their labour is in vain who build it.
Unless the Lord watches over the city,
In vain the guard keeps vigil. *R.*

It is in vain that you rise so early and go to bed so late;
Vain, too, to eat the bread of toil,
For he gives his belovèd sleep. *R.*

© *Society of St Francis 1992*
*Celebrating Common Prayer (Mowbray)*

## Psalm 50

*R:* Hear, O my people, and I will speak:
For I am God, your God.

Hear, O my people, and I will speak:
'O Israel, I will bear witness against you;
for I am God, your God.
I do not accuse you because of your sacrifices;
Your offerings are always before me. *R.*

'I will take no bull-calf from your stalls,
Nor he-goats out of your pens;
For the beasts of the forest are mine,
The herds in their thousands upon the hills.
I know every bird in the sky,
And the creatures of the fields are in my sight. *R.*

'If I were hungry, I would not tell you,
for the whole world is mine and all that is in it.
Do you think I eat the flesh of bulls,
Or drink the blood of goats?
Offer to God a sacrifice of thanksgiving
And make good your vows to the Most High.
Call upon me in the day of trouble;
I will deliver you and you shall honour me.' *R.*

*The following hymns (see chapter 14) may be used as litanies:*

'**Give thanks**' p81
'**All for you**'/'Peace for Me p92/93

# 5

# Sermon Material

This section contains outline sermons from different people with varying approaches to the subject for various occasions and seasons. They should not be followed slavishly, but used as a source of ideas. Giving and worship are so interwoven within the Christian message that many Bible readings are suitable starting points for preaching.

Something from this section should fit in most situations, but it is vital for any preacher to speak from the heart and out of their own experience.

## Enriched by Giving: 1 Timothy 6:17–19

At the heart of the gospel is generosity. Today we think about giving. The challenge is to respond to the gospel, not to find new and more enterprising ways of dabbling in fundraising. Our giving will enrich us, not least because it will liberate us from captivity to the power of money.

Money is understood by everyone, but in many churches the subject is taboo. But this should not be so. According to the scriptures, we have been created to carry on economic activity, to plant, to sow, to reap, to build shelters, to develop the fruit of the earth in all its many forms. In all this, money has come to be the medium of exchange, a convenience. It is not dirty – what is dirty, as St Paul reminds Timothy, is 'love of money', and that's different. The question is, how shall we handle what we have?

God gives – that is the basis of our faith; and he gives not because we deserve but because he loves what he has made. This is the heart of the gospel. As Christians our attitude to giving will be stunted until we recognize that God loves us. It is this truth about the love of God that we are in business to proclaim. That is our mission, that is the good news. We are here today because we know we are sinners and we need the love of God to put things right.

The God who made us and against whom we rebel is the same God who loves us. How can his love and judgement be reconciled? This is what the coming of Jesus is all about. This is what his cross signifies. He has taken what I deserve and transformed it, exchanged it – and God raised him. We are to accept that exchange, that gift.

So our giving of every aspect of our lives, including our money, is to be seen not as motivated by merit, but by thanksgiving in response to the generosity of a God who gives and loves to give. We need to give in order to reflect our new nature and our new life in Christ. As we come under his Lordship we will want to bring every-thing before him, including our monetary affairs. For as we learn to give, reflecting his self-giving, we are enriched.

Christians have a responsibility for resourcing God's mission through their church community. For the Church is God's idea – all those whose hearts have been touched by the gospel who should be seeking to share that with others. That's our mission: 'One beggar showing another where they can find bread.'

So giving through the local church to support ministry and mission is essential. It's a very practical response to God's giving. It's an acknowledgement that the earth is the Lord's, that we are grateful for our new life in Christ, that the proper use of our possessions is of interest to God – Jesus has much to say on this matter – and it is also a practical response to our desire to share with others.

If I think this way then a token offering simply will not do. I have to ask myself: How does the amount I give compare with what I'm prepared to pay for a meal out, for my newspapers, for stocking the drinks cabinet, for holidays, for a bigger car, for feeding the dog, for stocking the wardrobe? What does it say about me, my attitude to Christ's gospel, my commitment to the mission of God?

So how do we give? Our giving should be regular, not just when we feel like it. It should be a proportion of what we have at our disposal. A meaningful proportion. A noticeable proportion. A generous proportion. A sacrificial proportion. Our giving should be decided upon 'off the top', not out of the leftovers. Many of us need to abandon the practice of simply adjusting our giving on the basis of what was done in previous years and undergo a complete revolution in our attitude in obedience to God's word.

This word may be hard for some – I believe God wants to be heard by his people in this church in order that his Church might be empowered and enriched. Not impoverished, but enriched by a new turning in love and generosity to him who first loved us and constantly pours out from the riches of his grace even on such undeserving souls as you and me.

*Canon Barrie Gauge*

## Stewardship Sunday in Lent

The themes of Lent bring us face to face with the toughness of the gospel. It's not a bad time to be thinking about the stewardship of money – one of the hardest things to face about the teaching of Jesus. So many of our plans and aspirations are to do with money. If we can get our attitudes to money sorted out, how much happier we will be.

Stewardship Sunday is a very important day in the life of a church. Why? Is it to pay the quota, heating bills, insurance, repairs, etc., etc.? These things are important and it's very bad witness if they aren't dealt with properly. But money is important for even more basic and profound reasons:

• Money is an important factor in our lives. We spend a lot of time thinking about where it's coming from and where it's going. (*Give your own examples.*) If we believe in a loving God – then we must also believe that God cares about our money preoccupations. God cares about how we handle our money and possessions.

Yet so often the Church's handling of money and possessions leads to bad publicity and bad witness to the world. People have a very sharp nose for hypocrisy; they know when we don't practise what we preach. And it's no good blaming others: the diocese, synod, whoever. I am the Church. You are the Church. We are the Church.

I can do something about this. I can say to myself: I can't be true to Christ and keep my faith and my money separate, in different compartments of life where never the twain shall meet. Life's not like that. Reality will break in. And Jesus is a realist. He knows what my attitudes are. He knows what's going on in my heart of hearts, and he *cares*.

- My faith won't let me ignore this crucial subject of money. It speaks to me of a God who is intimately involved in creation, of a God who mysteriously initiated the material world, who is not pie in the sky but cares about the everyday, the here and now. It speaks to me of a God who is Word made flesh, who is eternity here in the present, who shows us that, through love, every aspect of our lives has meaning.

  It speaks to me of a God who takes every aspect of life on board, onto himself – and redeems it, sets it free, to be what it should be. And so, conforming to the risen life of Christ, struggling to follow in the way of Christ, wrestling with what it means to take up my cross and follow will affect my daily life. It will be real in the area of money and possessions.

  The nature of Christian faith is love. Love poured out in giving. 'God loved the world so much that he gave his only Son . . .' In Christ we see that love, that giving, and we respond in the only way we can, in worship and thanksgiving. This is where our thinking about giving must start. The nature of our faith leaves no other course, none that begins properly to honour our Saviour God; none that gives any hope of offering proper witness to the world.

- We have to be practical. Money is a practical subject. It is very good for getting things done. And so giving can and should be a practical expression of love, a sacramental expression of love, even. So giving should be thoughtful and generous, if it is to honour God and our neighbour, if it's to be realistic in the way our practical faith demands.

I can't be offhand or casual. I've got to pray about it and think about it. I have to decide in a way which gives God and God's work due priority in my life. My giving has to be proportionate. It's got to relate to the rest of my life. In proportion to my wealth, to my income, to what I spend (where my treasure is . . .). My giving needs to be appropriate for my circumstances.

Everybody's circumstances are different and God cares about how we handle *all* our possessions, not just what we give in church. But what we give in church needs to say something about whole lives lived for God. For many of us that will mean that our giving will strive towards the sacrificial – a difficult and challenging concept but part of the essence of Christian giving.

- How I handle my money, what I do about giving, cannot be separated from my worship of Almighty God. If God is sovereign in my life, commanding my worship, my prayer, my thanksgiving, my love, then my money and my giving will be subject to God and part of my spiritual life.

  And so we make decisions about our giving and pledge it to God, we offer a regular commitment as part of our worship, as a sign of our longing to practise what we preach.

As we handle money, as we decide about our giving, then our worship, our prayer, our thanksgiving to God in every Eucharist can be made firm and real. And the life of the Church really can be made a light for the world.

## The Sundays of Easter

We may not agree on *exactly* what happened 2000 years ago but there can be no doubt about what happened to the disciples. A group of ordinary, demoralized men were transformed by the events of that first Easter. Here was a group of people that was getting larger day by day, living out their Christian life with courage and boldness in the light of the resurrection. As faithful Christian people those events are life-changing for us as well.

Christ's death and resurrection give us a new status. As a colleague of mine puts it, Christians are 'has beens' – we *have been* where the world still is. As Christians, we've been moved on by the events of Easter.

In the letter to the Ephesians the writer describes the sinful environment in which we existed. Our status was nothing and we got what we deserved.

But God, who is rich in mercy, out of the great love with which he loved us even when we were dead through our trespasses, made us alive together with Christ – by grace you have been saved – and raised us up with him.

*(Ephesians 2:4–6a)*

Our status is that we have *already* been raised up. We are set apart to be God's demonstration model of his love.

For by grace you have been saved through faith, and this is not your own doing; it is the gift of God – not the result of works, so that no one may boast. For we are what he has made us.

*(Ephesians 2:8–10a)*

Whatever we are it's not primarily as a result of what we've done. Our status with God is all of *his* doing. When we begin to realize and believe and experience this 'has-been-ness', then we can begin to understand that

- all that we have is of God, and in that sense
- everything that we have belongs to him, because without him we have nothing.

This is in a nutshell what discipleship – our following of Jesus, our active response as Temples of the Holy Spirit and as members of the body of Christ – is all about. These are all metaphors of close involvement and they require practical action in response to God's action.

Our response is the giving of ourselves – and the most difficult part of ourselves to give is our money. But it's an issue that we must address from time to time and it's not one we should shy away from. But we shouldn't think of it in terms of dragging something out of people to pay the bills. Set in its proper context, the impetus for Christian giving is that response to God.

It's a response in the giving of

- ourselves – in worship, Bible reading and prayer;
- our time in meeting the needs of others;
- our skills in giving back to God for his purposes the special things that make us what we are;
- our money to fund not only his mission in our local church but also the work that he calls us to do with one another in our communities at home and overseas.

Archbishop George Carey has put it like this:

The spirit of generosity calls us to give joyfully and sacrificially. The first question to ask is not 'what do I need to give?' but 'how can my giving reflect something of God's love for me?'

But as Christians we have to take a step of faith to move into such a life-changing way of living. Such a step of faith will

- allow us to plan our giving to God and his Church first, before we pay other bills;
- allow us to give in proportion to our income;
- allow us to trust in God that we *can* give regularly and sacrificially;
- allow us to believe that it's not the end of the world if the Church receives more than it needs – that's in fact the beginning of the growth of the kingdom.

The response that we're called to make is summed up in the last verse of the Good Friday hymn:

Were the whole realm of nature mine,
  that were an offering far too small;
love so amazing, so divine,
  demands my soul, my life, my all.

We have within our grasp the opportunity to make a serious difference to the Church's mission. As we reflect on the changed lives of the disciples after the resurrection, let us pray that we will make the connection with a renewed response in our lives.

### Christian Aid Week: Matthew 25:31–46

Mother Teresa of Calcutta has said, 'The biggest disease today is not leprosy or TB, but the feeling of being unwanted and uncared for. The greatest evil in the world is the terrible indifference towards one's neighbour.'

It would be easy to ignore this reading from Matthew. Unless you are the clergy, people don't turn up on your doorstep wanting food and drink. Nor, even for us, naked. Three exclusions such as these could make us feel we are let off the hook.

Perhaps we need to reshape them.

- The King will say get away from me, for I was hungry: hungry for a smile and all I got was sour looks. Hungry for encouragement and all you did was point out my mistakes.
- I was thirsty for a word of recognition, but you ignored me. Thirsty for a bit of companionship, but you passed me by.
- I was a stranger: just someone a bit different, and you refused to have anything to do with me. I was a child and you wouldn't let your children play with me.
- I was naked, not because I had no clothes, but because I lacked a sense of self-worth and you dismissed me from your attention.
- I was sick, sick from doubt and worry, and you never even noticed. Sunk in a pit of despair, and you said it was all my own fault.
- I was in prison, not one of iron bars, but a prison of nerves, of loneliness, and you gave me the cold shoulder.

I imagine that none of us could put our hand on our heart and come out of that unscathed.

To give gratefully and generously with money and energy to alleviate the real and desperate needs of people at home and abroad is a vital part of our calling. But the motivation to do so has its roots in our more domestic relationships, for no one is an island entire of itself, as the poet John Donne reminded us. To be fully human we need to keep the two calls together: our solidarity with those a safe distance away needs to be balanced with the almost more taxing duty to those all too close.

By baptism we have a solidarity with the life of God, but we immediately inherit a large family of people we have never seen and never met. That brings apparently daunting commitments, but can also, if we let it, be a source of enrichment. Can we value that?

## The Ten Lepers: Luke 17:11–19

'Human kind cannot bear very much reality' (T. S. Eliot, *Four Quartets*). Perhaps that is why the Old Testament prophets tended to have a hard time. They were sharp and attentive to the reality of relationships, especially economic relationships. Mend your ways, they said, you who victimize the poor. Remember God is on the side of the poor, the orphan, the widow, the alien. This is not a popular message with the rich and powerful.

The reality of the Christian message can be hard for us to face up to and to live up to, but to commit to the attempt can be a liberation. It is actually very important to act on the message. Practise what you preach, otherwise it is no earthly use. The Christian message, and Christian worship, has at its heart the idea of thanksgiving: what can it mean to put this into practice?

The famous story of the ten lepers is about thanksgiving. They all plead for help, they all are helped, but only one turns round to give thanks. And that is the Samaritan, the least acceptable one. This can serve as a model of what the Church is about. God's love is for all, but not many give thanks, not many come to worship and praise God. This can make us rather sad and fed up. But should this be the case? Would you rather be that one leper, or one of the other nine?

Being here, in worship, in thanksgiving, is what it is all about, is what enables us to move onward and outward.

Thanksgiving is the key – it is not a woolly emotion. It is the keynote, the basic attitude for Christians to take out from worship into the rest of their lives. 'Get up and go on your way,' says Jesus to the leper, but go on your way changed by what I have done for you. 'Your faith has made you well'; go on with your life trusting in me. Stay well, in your attitudes and in your actions.

It's got to be put into practice, in the real world – in the world where money is important. Perhaps this, too, is not a popular message, but it is a vital one. Think of the story of the conversion of the Danes to Christianity: when they were baptized, they would hold their swords out of the water so that that bit remained unconverted. Obviously completely wrongheaded, but do we not tend to do that with our purses and wallets, bank accounts and credit cards? Do we not tend to hold these out of the water of new life?

We don't face up to the fact that Jesus knows what we are up to. He knows this about us. He is realistic, even if we are not. Look how realistic Jesus is about money throughout the Gospels. He knows how much our handling of money says about us, and about our relationships, with God and with each other.

Often we are depressed because the Church seems short of money. But this is simply reality catching up with us. We are wealthy compared with most of those who have lived, or do live, in the world. And we are the Church: the Church is not short of money, it is just that Church members do not care to put it in the common purse. This is a great opportunity: facing reality is what the Christian faith is meant to be about.

This is the reality of where the Church is today. Money is important. Hiding is no longer an option. Facing the reality of money means thinking about giving. This may not be something we are used to. Nevertheless, the likelihood is that soon there will be two sorts of Church.

There will be 'one leper' churches where generous and sacrificial giving is the norm, where people give proportionately of what they have – a twelfth, a tenth, a fifth; where commitments to regular giving are made and then devotedly carried out. Such churches will be happy, forward looking, positive, thankful. And there will be churches where the love of God is not expressed in such a way, churches that struggle and moan and resent the cost of discipleship; churches that, like the nine lepers, do not return to give thanks. Only we can decide which way to go, but it seems clear to me which would be more fun.

## Harvest Thanksgiving

These celebrations which come once a year tell us what we ought to be celebrating all the time but sometimes forget.

Harvest Thanksgiving is a nudge to remember that we need to be very grateful for what we have and not forget where it comes from. We are reminded that God is the creator and provider of all things and that we are called to thank him, and we are called to work with him.

We all know that Eucharist means 'thanksgiving'. Here, day by day, week by week, we praise God as creator. We thank him for his love as shown in the life, death and resurrection of Jesus. We offer the self-giving and sacrifice of Jesus and receive a share in his new life.

Thanking and sacrifice go together: the alternative is to be miserly. We know from books, stories and our own experience that mean and miserly people are not happy people. Their vision is mean and miserly in every way. They spread a deadening, diminishing effect.

It is, of course, easy to see other people as miserly and fail to spot the signs in ourselves. God does not want us to be mean and miserly. He wants us to live life to the full, and that means living thankfully.

On the issue of whether Christians are better than non-believers, Archbishop Robert Runcie once said, 'Oh dear no, they're not, but they carry about with them a sense of thankfulness.' Do we, the Church today, carry about a sense of thankfulness?

Deep down we would like to; we know life would be better if we did. Rather like St Teresa of Avila, I don't love God, I don't want to love God, but I do want to want to love God.

What about thankfulness in daily life, in the mundane details of work, home and Church? Although we are called to co-operate with God, although we are to that extent in control of our lives, we know very well that there is that other element – the imponderable, the inspirational, the holy, call it what we will – where we can only pause in silence and humility and even thankfulness.

If we look at our deepened understanding of how things are, our health and wealth, our relationships, we can find that whatever snags we might encounter, there is always something to be thankful for, if we have that gracious ability to recognize it.

Thankfulness does not come naturally. We have to be taught it at an early age and then learn that it does not end with mouthing the words. Thankfulness is shown by the way we live, by the relationships we develop. Thankfulness is shown by giving.

Giving shows that we can share, wanting others to have something of what has been given to us. Harvest reminds us that such giving comes out of thankfulness for what we can do, under God, in co-operation with others. Without thankfulness, communities become sour and lifeless.

It is only by giving, perhaps with some effort of will, that we become the sort of people we would like everybody else to be: generous, selfless, loving, supportive.

To give helps us to remain thankful. Every weekly offering reminds us of our blessings. There is so much that is good in creation, in life, in the Church. Our worship is the time to make our response of thankfulness for that, for our own lives, and all that is to follow.

## Christ the King

Old Testament    Ezekiel 34:11–16, 20–24
Psalm            Psalm 95:1–7a
New Testament    Ephesians 1:15–23
The Gospel       Matthew 25:31–46

*(Common Worship – Year A readings)*

This last Sunday in the Church's year is a good time to have a look at ourselves so that we can make the necessary changes and get ourselves ready for the new year. It's a good time for preparation and, as a part of that, it's a good time to look at our giving.

Our giving as Christian people involves much more than money – it involves giving the whole self to God. And our whole selves are everything that we have and everything that we are – our time, our strengths, our weaknesses, and our money. And our giving is not just 10% or 5% – it can be nothing short of 100% that we offer to God as our Christian duty and service.

Today we celebrate 'Christ the King', and what a good opportunity that gives us to look at the reason and motivation for our giving. This theme gives a glorious climax to the end of our Church year and the picture of Christ the King on the throne in his kingdom leads naturally to Advent and the theme of judgement. At the end of the Church's year we catch a glimpse of the kingdom for which we're called to work and pray.

It's in response to that picture and recognizing our part in it as members of Christ's body that we see the context for our giving. In the world outside the Church we hear the message: 'This is what it costs – will you help us pay the bills?' That's not the motivation for Church people – we don't look first to the bills.

Christian giving is primarily a response by faithful people to a loving and generous God, who's given us all that we have. Christian giving is a theological matter. Our money becomes almost a sacrament and our giving of a proportion of our money or anything else is a token that dedicates the whole. Christian giving is a natural part of discipleship and it's at the heart of our walk with Christ.

Our psalm and readings today give us different pictures of Christ the King. We hear about:

• God the creator. This is where our responsibility as stewards of all that God has given us begins. We're called to act responsibly with God's creation and we have to give an account of our stewardship. God has made us and all that we are and that demands a proportion of our time and our service and our money to be set aside for his work.
• God the shepherd who loves and cares. God in Christ cares for his

people and the nature of that relationship is of a shepherd to his sheep. He gives himself first to us. Giving by Christians follows from giving ourselves first back to the Lord as we seek to be more like our heavenly father.

- Christ who is risen in glory to be with the father. Here we have a picture of Christ in majesty. That's the picture we need to have in our minds when we think of how on earth we can respond to such a God. Our giving has to be sacrificial and generous but it's also appropriate that it's proportionate to what we have. This is not the place for guilt or anxiety but a cheerful response after prayer and reflection.

- Christ the King in judgement. When have we seen Christ in need and have failed to come to his aid? Surely we wouldn't do such a thing! But we see Christ in each other and when we meet each other's needs then we are meeting Christ's needs.

Truly I tell you, just as you did it to one of the least of these who are members of my family, you did it to me.

*(Matthew 25:40)*

This is the mission of the Church. If you just look at your giving and try to discover what you get back for it – a kind of supermarket mentality – then you'll find cheerful and sacrificial giving a great strain and a source of anxiety.

But our giving is to resource the mission of the Church and a part of that is the way we treat each other in our Christian community. By my giving of money others can minister in places that I can't be. My giving helps to enable the Church's response to those in need.

We give because that's one way we have of directly expressing our thanksgiving to God for his gifts. The motive for giving is to give because we've been given to. Giving is our thankful response to God who's given so much to us. Giving is our response to our God who we see in majesty as Christ the King.

On this last Sunday of the Church's year the Church has used the collect: 'Stir up, O Lord, the wills of your faithful people . . .'

Let us pray that as we think through our own giving to the mission of the Church that our wills will be stirred and that we will be bold and brave enough to respond as God is calling us.

## Outline for a Series of Sermons

*1  Believing and trusting in God*

- *Ways of thinking about God*
  The God of creation, of the Old Testament, of popular belief. The Bible is a whole library of books about God's relationship with his people. The God of the Bible is a developing concept.
- *Our God is a God of relationship*
  A relationship of trust. Believing in God means more than just thinking God exists: it means trusting in him.
- *God of community*
  The comedian Dave Allen ends his act by saying 'May your God go with you'. But is God an individualistic concept we each create for ourselves? Surely 'No' – our God relates to a community. The Bible tells us about that relationship. Our God loves the world and the whole of creation.
- *God of creation*
  The power and beauty of creation. The energy and commitment revealed in creation. This is costly – not just a chocolate-box image.
- *The problem of evil*
  What of 'nature red in tooth and claw'? The problem of suffering? The orthodox answer to this is 'free will'. But what of the natural suffering in creation itself? In the end this remains a mystery.
- *The vision of God with us*
  In Christianity our relationship with God addresses that mystery. We are given a new, special, unique vision of what God is like. God is seen to be at one with us and in creation. God confronts the evil in us and the suffering in creation.
- *Recreation*
  The costliness of the creation is matched by the costliness of the recreation: all is made whole in the life, the death and the resurrection of Christ. Christ is at one with us in everything that happens in our lives.

## 2  Following Christ

- *The God of all things comes into our lives through Christ*
  'God so loved the world that he gave his only Son' Jesus Christ. God's generosity, giving and love are fully expressed in Christ.
- *We are the recipients of that love*
  We do not deserve to receive that love, but it is poured out for us freely. This is transforming – life can never be the same again – and to say anything else is to belittle the love we have received.
- *This must be the basis of our response*
  Our lives must be transformed by the realization of what has been done for us. Our hearts and attitudes must be transformed by the overwhelming generosity shown to us. We must overflow with gratitude and thanksgiving. Nothing else will do, it is the foundation to which we must always return.
- *The content of our response*
  We are compelled towards Christ. Christ who has transformed us and our way of looking at life. Christ, the model of true humanity. Christ, the Way, the Truth and the Life. It's all summed up in Christ's expression of generous, outflowing love.
- *Christ's vocation*
  The Gospels tell us of Christ's awareness of the inevitable outcome of living out his vocation. Loving and giving will include the ultimate sacrifice of the cross.
- *The difficulty they felt and we feel*
  The disciples are reluctant to receive or accept this knowledge. We have the same difficulty in taking the implications into our own lives. It *is* difficult to follow one who has turned the world's values upside down, who has put the first last and the last first, who has become the servant and the least of all to become the saviour of all.
- *Outrageous love*
  What is powerful and honoured by conventional society, by conventional religion or in our own lives – all this is as nothing beside the outrageous love which is lavished upon us by Christ.
- *The way of love*
  This love is so strong and powerful that it can only be

transforming – it must make a difference in our lives. It can only lead to the desire and longing to follow in the way of the one who is the source of such love. In the shadow of the cross, the only way to live is generously.

## 3  Worshipping God in his Church

We have thought of God in relationship with people and creation, who has reached out to us in the great love of Christ. This leads us to respond, to follow along the same way.

- *The desire to worship*
  This is also part of our response. Thomas' response to the risen Christ, 'My Lord and my God!' (John 20:28), is primarily an act of worship, and it takes place in the context of the emergent Christian community, where and for which the Eucharist has been instituted. Thomas is the person for us and for our time. He longs for more certainty, for his questions to be answered, for life to be sorted, for problems to be solved.
- *Truly human response*
  In the end, however, he is driven to his knees in worship. In the face of the crucified and risen Christ, worship is the only response that rings true. This is the only response appropriate for any human being to make. A response which acknowledges our sin, failure and compromise. We fall to our knees in worship of the Son of God, who has, by his sacrificial love, saved us from ourselves and given us the chance to be what we were created to be.
- *Commemoration*
  The commemoration of this is at the heart of Christian worship. It is at the heart of the Eucharist (thanksgiving) which is central to our worship, the corporate action of the Church, the body of Christ.
- *Thanksgiving*
  We are compelled to give thanks. We long to give thanks for creation and recreation, for Christ's loving and giving, for God's saving love for us. We give thanks that God's presence with us

is focused in the ordinary, simple created things of bread and wine. We give thanks that we have been called to follow in this way.

- *Not an end in itself*
  We give thanks that this Christian worship is not an end in itself, but enables us to go out into the world as the body of Christ to be Christ for, and to see Christ in, all who come our way.

## 4  *Money and possessions are given by God*

- *The God of all things*
  To believe and trust in God, to worship and follow Christ, are ideas we are used to affirming. Our first three sermons have simply said that God is the God of all things. If that is so, then it should not be too difficult to say also that money and possessions are given by God and should be used accordingly.
- *Money and Possessions*
  But money and possessions? They're mine! Once we get beyond the warm glow of generalities, it's not so easy. Christians do indeed have difficulty with Christ's message about possessions. This has always been the case, as the Gospels reveal. (*Select your own examples from Jesus' sayings and one-to-one encounters about money and possessions.*)
- *The history of the Church*
  The same difficulty is seen in the history of the Church, in the debates about usury and the holding of wealth. We can see it in our current concerns (*give a relevant example*). But this should not be the case.
- *Christianity's unique message*
  We have our doctrines of creation and incarnation. In Christianity the material is vital to the spiritual. This should make Christianity the ideal creed for dealing with money and possessions.
- *Redemption of all things*
  As God redeems us by coming into our lives in Jesus, so is redeemed all that we are and all that we have. All is made as it should be once more, so as to be used as it should be once more.

God has made what we are and what we have. Jesus has remade what we are and what we have – this is the Good News.

- *With Good News goes responsibility*
  All we are and all we have is remade, and with outrageous generosity, divine generosity, it is handed back to us, unconditionally. Christian faith is an adult faith. We are given the responsibility. And we can do what we like with it.
- *The challenge of responsibility*
  We can explode weapons of enormous power. We can wage war. We can foul up the environment. I can ignore the poor and the outcast and choose instead to look after number one. Or I can behave in accordance with what I say I believe, and place what I am and what I have and what I do before my God. That's not so comfortable, but it is what I am called to do and, in the end, it is what I'll be happiest trying to do.

## 5  Giving meaningfully in worship

- *The challenge hits home*
  If I accept that God has made all things and that, in Jesus, he has shown his infinite love for what he has made, then I know that my life, money and possessions must be part of that, along with everything else. But it really hits home when I have to think about my giving, and the challenge affects my real life in the real world. Here is Jesus' great challenge to my heart and my attitude, to my relationship with God and with my fellow men and women.
- *Pharisees*
  St Luke tells us that the Pharisees didn't like what Jesus had to say, that they loved money and so scoffed and jeered at him (16:14). That is no more than we expect: we are conditioned to the Pharisees getting it wrong and we don't think it has much to do with us. But we do well to remember that the Pharisees were those who took their religion very seriously, who had most in common with Jesus.
- *Just like us*
  In our terms, they were the ones most like us: keen on Church, moral values, doing the right thing. What happens if we substitute

ourselves for the Pharisees? 'The **Christians**, who were lovers of money, heard all this, and they ridiculed him!' How does that fit?

- *Jesus knows us and loves us*
  He knows that loving money, avarice, greed, possessiveness, clinging on to what we've got, is a universal human condition. This is particularly relevant to the times in which we live. Jesus knows all of this, he is a realist: 'Where your treasure is, there will your heart be also' (Matthew 6:21).

- *Spiritual reality*
  This is a spiritual matter. Jesus knows and loves us in the real world. He knows what is in our hearts and attitudes. Our response must be shown by real actions in the real world. It's not easy to respond, but it has to be done. Otherwise our faith becomes unreal, a fantasy and an escape.

- *Response in worship*
  Our thanksgiving, our prayer, our worship means offering what we are, what we have, what we own, what we spend, what we save, what we give away, to God.

- *The stewardship of money is crucial to this*
  This is not just about the needs of God's people (2 Corinthians 9:12). Much more than that, it is about how Christians live their lives. It's about knowing we will always be rich enough to be generous. It's about realizing that generosity breeds thanksgiving, which breeds more generosity in ourselves and in others.

- *Testing the reality of faith*
  It's also about realizing that how we deal with money is a test of the reality of our faith. This is something we have to think, pray and decide about. Every Christian should offer before God their stewardship of money. That must include putting money into the common purse of the Church, so that God's work can be done, and giving money away, so that God's creation can be cared for and his people loved.

- *Keeping things in proportion*
  Giving is the acid test, and it should be proportionate. Proportionate to what we have, to what our income is, to what we spend on other things. The proportion we offer at the Lord's table

represents the whole, all we have and all we are. What that proportion is says a lot about how important God is in our lives.

- *Meaningful giving*

  If I give a meaningful amount of money as part of my worship, I am putting into practice my faith's call to me to love, thank and serve God. And I free myself to love myself and others as God calls me to. And to do that together as a worshipping community is a powerful sign of love in God's world.

# 6

# All-age Worship

The principles of Christian stewardship are not a subject that should be exclusive to adult worship. Often adults can better understand them if they are put over at all-age worship.

The teaching of Christian stewardship as a part of the separate activities for children and young people is outside the scope of this book. Many other publications provide outline lessons and activities.

The preaching or activities at all-age worship can cover the themes of

- receiving – all that we have comes from a generous God. Do we mean *all*?
- generosity – God's generosity deserves a generous response, but with what?
- sharing – who do we love so that we share what we have with them?
- giving – we have a responsibility to respond to God, through his Church, but how much?

The best way to handle these themes will depend on

- the way a stewardship programme is being conducted for adults and its themes;
- the season in the Church's year;
- the nature of the congregation and the age of the children;
- the ability of the building space to allow interactive worship with activities, questions and answers.

The important thing is to engage with the children by starting from their experience of life and making connections with the Christian life and Christian stewardship. Use can be made of appropriate images and characters that they see on television or that connect with life in the locality about which they are aware. Use dialogue and visual aids so that there is a real learning experience. At times it may be better to break the sermon slot down into two or three shorter sessions, which may engage better with shorter attention spans.

*Example 1*

*Making the connection between saying thank you for what we're given for our birthday and saying thank you to God at harvest time for the things we're given by God.*

Imagine it's your birthday and a relation who lives some distance away has given you £10. How do you thank them? A good way would be to write a thank-you letter.

Let's pretend to do it now. What would we say?

Dear . . . . . . .

Thank you for giving me £10 for my birthday.
I will use it for . . . . . .

Then you might tell them how you're getting on at school . . .

With love from . . . . . . .

Summary

- We say thank you.
- We say how we are going to use the gift.
- We say how we're getting on.

Today it's harvest festival when we thank God for his goodness through the harvest. But it's also a good time to thank him for *all* his goodness to us.

So what would we say to God if we wrote him a letter?

Dear God,
Thank you for all the good things you give us each day.

(The special thing about God is that we have a special relationship with him. So, as his children, we have to look after the things he gives us and use them in the way he wants us to use them.

He asks us to use some of what he gives us by giving it back to him. We give back in order to say thank you for what he has given us. So how might we use his gifts? We could spend time helping others, try to do good deeds, or give some money to help his work.)

With love from . . . . . . .

That's the message of harvest. We thank God for what he's given us and we give some of what he's given us back to him so that the work of the Church can continue.

## Example 2

*Focusing on the special things we have in life and how we use the things that we have.*

Invite people to bring something that is special to them to the service (this can be done through the invitations, Sunday School and notices). Make it clear that this is not just for the children.

At the appointed time ask people to hold up what they have brought. Those who haven't brought anything could be invited to think of something special and raise their hand.

Ask a few people what they have brought and why it is special to them. Include questions such as where did they get it from, was it a gift, did they buy it, did they make it? Try to pick a mixture of children and adults.

Explain that we all have things that are so special to us and this is something to rejoice in and celebrate. We also celebrate the fact that all that we have is given to us by God, who wants us to enjoy and use the things that we have, not just for ourselves but for the good of others.

Our time is special. We use our time to make our living. God calls us to think about how we use our time not just for ourselves but for others.

What we are good at is special. We all have something unique to give, to do, to make, to offer. If possible give examples from the special items focused on earlier. God calls us to think about how we use our gifts.

Money is a gift. We all rely on it to live. Often no matter how much we have it doesn't seem enough. But we know how good it feels when someone buys us something special – again use some of the examples if possible.

Our money is a gift from God and we are called to give thanks for it and then think about what we do with it. God's generosity calls for our generous response.

You might like to end with everyone holding up the special things that they have brought and saying a short prayer thanking God for them, for all the special things in our lives and asking him to help us to use what we have for his purpose.

## Example 3

*A helpful story for harvest about our responsibility to give back to God, that can be demonstrated visually.*

There once was a man and God gave him ten apples. God told him to put one apple aside to give back in thanks to God.

God also told him he could exchange

- three apples for food;
- three apples for a house to live in;
- and three apples for some clothes to wear.

He took the first three apples to a supermarket and exchanged them for a trolleyload of all the nicest food he could eat. Then he took three apples to a high-street store and exchanged them for suits of clothes. He took three apples to an estate agent and exchanged them for a lovely house in this area. (*Names of local shops can be used.*)

Then he saw that he only had one apple left. He remembered that God had said that he must give an apple back in thanksgiving, but he knew that God had made the world and that God owned everything and surely God could manage without this small, insignificant apple? So he ate it and gave God the core.

Do we plan for God first or do we give only when we see what we have got left over?

## Example 4

*A story to demonstrate receiving and giving and that we only become the people we should be when we do both.*

The land of Israel encompasses two major bodies of water. In the northern part of the country is the Sea of Galilee, fed by the River Jordan as it flows from Mount Hermon southward. Teeming with life, this lake is a symbol of the richness of the land. Fish are so plentiful that they provide the area with its major industry, as well as the main component of its diet.

Not only in the lake, but all around it as well, are the signs of the rich blessing it offers to the land: lush green estates and pasture with grass and trees in incredible abundance. The cool, fresh water is the gift of God to a thirsty country, and it enriches the whole area.

Leaving the Sea of Galilee, the Jordan meanders on down the valley toward the southern end of the country, still fresh, still rich with life as it passes along.

But only 60 miles south the Jordan feeds into another lake, strangely opposite to the Sea of Galilee in every way. In this one, nothing lives at all. Around it there is no greenery, no growth of any kind. Even those trees that once grew close enough to be touched by the lake's influence are gaunt ghosts of life, stark skeletons of trees encrusted and strangled by the salt that cakes everything.

Any observer is compelled to ask what has happened to the water in a few short miles. How could it be so rich and full of life and yet so barren when it reaches the Dead Sea? The answer is that nothing has happened to the water itself. Analysis of the Jordan just before it enters the Dead Sea would show its water to be just as good as further north.

But the Dead Sea has no outlet. Its level is maintained only through evaporation. Everything it receives it keeps for itself, and the result is a dreadful kind of death.

If we keep the things of God for ourselves, then we too suffer a kind of slow death to the world. If we use the things of God to love him and to love our neighbour and to bless the world, then we will grow and flourish.

# 7

# Reflection and Meditation

Your hands, Lord, like your heart,
are always open,
ready to embrace, keen to bless.

The table you lay groans with good things;
the cup you fill overflows;
. . . and this is not for the expected guests,
 but for the last and the least,
 for those whom the world has shown
 no generosity.

Make my hands and my heart,
 my table and my wallet
 well worn, like yours,
 with love.

© *Panel on Worship*
*Church of Scotland*

Lord Jesus
for you money is not a dirty commodity,
the stuff of private conversations,
the enemy of all that is spiritual.

You handled coins, paid taxes,
acknowledged the realities of trade and commerce,
and were unafraid to identify and condemn
the misuse, the false security, and the lure of money.

Through your Holy Spirit,
inform the consciences of all who govern our finances,
   fix trade prices,
   raise interest rates or cancel debt.
May money and morality never be kept poles apart
in national treasure or private homes;
and though your head does not appear on our coinage
may we use it as in your sight.

*© Panel on Worship*
*Church of Scotland*

God of all life,
in you is novelty and everlastingness,
   lavishness and simplicity.

In me, aware of the needs of humanity
   and of limitations of the earth,
there is confusion over what to buy,
   what to preserve,
   what to destroy,
   and how to be a good steward
   of your resources.

Because good works alone do not lead to salvation,
make me open to the prompting of your Holy Spirit.
Then may I live wisely and well.

*© Panel on Worship*
*Church of Scotland*

Save us Lord,
from the temptation to buy what we do not need;
from confusing what we need with what we want;
from wasting what we do not own,
from owning what we will never use,
from idealizing the past as a golden age;
from bequeathing our children a sorry inheritance.

Strengthen the arm and the will
of all who, for the good of the world you made and love,
challenge our greed
and inform us about appropriate living.
May their words gain a good hearing
so that the world may have a good future.

*© Panel on Worship*
*Church of Scotland*

Sparse sowing, meagre reaping;
but if we are generous, bountiful will be the harvest.
So let us give what we can,
not with regret, nor from a sense of duty.
God loves a cheerful giver.

And when we help others, we will not just meet their needs,
we will unleash a flood of gratitude to God.
Many will give glory to God
for our loyalty to the gospel and for our generosity.
God loves a cheerful giver.

*A New Zealand Prayer Book*
*Anglican Church in Aotearoa, New Zealand and Polynesia*

## Jesus

Jesus lived here on earth
A life of obedience
A life of giving
A life of worship.

Jesus died, doing his Father's will
An act of obedience
An act of giving
An act of worship.

Jesus lives through his Church
Lives of obedience
Lives of giving
Lives of worship.

The Church does the Father's will
Acts of obedience
Acts of giving
Acts of worship.

*© Frances Ballantyne*

## Partners of Love

| | |
|---|---|
| We love | because you first loved us |
| We give | because you gave yourself completely |
| We worship | because you showed your very nature |
| We live | because you died instead of us |
| We share | because your care surrounds us all |
| We love | because you first loved us. |

*© Frances Ballantyne*

## Divine Exchange

Jesus, we thank you.

In your generosity, you became poor for us,
In your giving, you became empty for us,
In your grace, you became nothing for us.

You became poor, for us to become rich,
You became empty, for us to become full,
You became nothing, for us to become something.

Jesus, we thank you.

*© Frances Ballantyne*

## Given in Love

In our collections, week by week,
From our purses, or by promised envelope,
Keep us cheerful in our giving.

At the gathering of the gifts, each time of worship,
From our pensions, or our housekeeping,
Keep us generous in our giving.

In our committed giving, reclaiming income tax,
From our earnings in our plenty,
Keep us humble in our giving.

*© Frances Ballantyne*

Forgive us Lord for the crumbs of comfort
that we offer to your starving world.
Forgive us for the self-indulgence
which is blind to the suffering of your children.
Forgive us for letting wealth and the desire to get rich
lead us into foolish and harmful behaviour.
Forgive us for thinking that one big win will sort out
    all our problems.
When we are blessed with worldly attributes,
keep us from showing off,
or thinking that we have achieved anything that you
    have not given us.
Teach us we pray to place our hope in the certainty of your love,
    to know how to use our wealth wisely and justly,
    to be rich in good works,
    to be generous and ready to share,
    to value the lives of those about us
and never let our lives be ruined by greed, envy, or pride.

For you are our God
from whom all life springs and to whom all life returns,
you are our wealth,
the harvest of all our labours,
bread for the hungry, sight for the blind,
freedom for the oppressed, hope for the desperate,
home for the homeless, security for the refugee,
and judge of how we live your life.

*© Colin Ferguson*
*(Based on Psalm 146, Luke 16:19–31, 1 Timothy 6:6–19)*

Generous God, you ask us to trust in you for everything.
But it's so hard to do that.
We've learned to trust the money in our pockets
to put a roof over our heads,
food on the table
and to provide all the luxuries we feel we can afford –
and some we can't.
It's difficult to know how we would manage otherwise.

Father, forgive us our lack of trust.
If we had no money we would have to depend on you.
Help us to remember this
and, with that knowledge,
to understand that you are depending on us
to be open-handed with what we have,
on your behalf,
towards those who are trusting
that you will provide for them.

*© Marjorie Dobson*

Jesus, when you lived on earth you didn't wear designer jeans, or labelled trainers, or carry luggage with the right name on it. You took the simple route, with practical clothes and no excess baggage.

Please help us to examine our values and priorities and to be aware of the message we give to others, if we insist on being as fashionable as they are.

Jesus, when you talked about money you praised those who gave sacrificially, challenged those who had too much money for their own good and urged people to be honest and to pay their due taxes.

Please forgive us those times when we are selfish in our use of money, believing that what we earn we are entitled to spend as we please. Keep us honest in our dealings and prompt us to generosity, as we respond to the needs of those who have nothing.

Jesus, you gave people your time and attention, dealing with each individual and their problems on a personal basis, even though you were aware of how much energy that drained from you.

Please strengthen us to face the demands that other people's needs place on our time and energy. Remind us that you never turn us away when we need you.

Jesus, your whole life was an example of giving to others.

Teach us how to be more like you.

*© Marjorie Dobson*

# 8

# Dialogues

## The Two-Pound Coin

A   Hey! There's a coin down here. It's a two-pound coin! That'll boost the collection this week. It'll look odd among all the pound coins and fifty-pences, but I'll put it in anyway.

B   Hey! You can't do that. It's mine!

A   How do you know that?

B   It's mine. It belongs to me. It came out of my pocket.

A   But it doesn't have your name on it.

B   Of course it doesn't. Don't be silly. It doesn't have anybody's name on it.

A   Yes it does. Look at it.

B   Where?

A   There! Round the face.

B   Oh, you mean the Queen. Yes, well it's got her name on it, of course.

A   So it means it belongs to her.

B   No it doesn't.

A   But it's got her name on it.

B   I know! But that's just because it's a British coin and she's the Queen.

A   So, it's not hers?

B   No!

A   Well it's got some other writing on it. Look! Round the edge.

B   (reading) 'Standing on the shoulders of giants.'

A   Then the coin belongs to the giants!

B   Now you're being really silly. There aren't any giants.

A   How about the giants of industry? Or commerce? The bankers?

That's it! The coin belongs to the bankers.

B    No it doesn't! It belongs to me. The bank gave it to me.

A    Why?

B    Because it was in my bank account. It was my money. I earned it. So it belongs to me.

A    But look! There's some more writing on it. It's in Latin.

B    Oh, this is ridiculous! Let's see. D-E-I G-R-A – oh, I can't be bothered with that. What does it mean?

A    Well. I know D-E-I spells Dei – that means God. That's it! The coin belongs to God!

B    No, it doesn't! The coin belongs to me. What on earth would God want with my money anyway?

A    Precisely! What on earth would God want to do with our money?

*© Marjorie Dobson*

## How Much Should I Give?

Voice 1    'Pay the emperor what belongs to the emperor and pay to God what belongs to God.'

Voice 2    What puzzles Jesus left for us to interpret. 'Pay the emperor what belongs to the emperor.' That's easy enough – pay my income tax to the government. I do that, even if I grumble about it.

Voice 1    What about the rest?

Voice 2    You mean what's left after I've paid the tax, the national insurance, the graduated pension, the union fees etc., etc.?

Voice 1    Yes, that bit. Is that God's, or yours?

Voice 2    Both I suppose, mine and God's. I give quite a lot to my church and my favourite charities. I also put money in the charity envelopes and give to special appeals and people collecting on the streets.

Voice 1    What about all those other charity requests that keep coming through your door?

Voice 2    Well, there's so many now. If they're not the ones I support regularly then I put them in the bin.

Voice 1    Even though you've just bought a new car?

| Voice 2 | But mine had just failed its MOT and it would have cost so much to repair that it seemed more sensible to put the money towards a new one. After all I do *need* a car. How could I give the old folk lifts to church, or provide transport for the Youth Club outing without one? |
|---|---|
| Voice 1 | OK, calm down, point taken. What about the holiday to Australia? |
| Voice 2 | Yes. So I'm going to Australia, but it's much more than a holiday. Our grandson is six months old and I haven't seen him yet. We've saved for a year for this by not going out to meals, or getting takeaways, except for birthdays and our wedding anniversary. I'm sure God understands this and doesn't expect me to give it all away. Does he? |
| Voice 1 | So what do you think Jesus means by 'Pay God what belongs to God'? |
| Voice 2 | He means that I should think of everything as being a loan from God – my money, my car, my holidays. They are for me to enjoy, but also to use to help others whenever I can. Even I really belong to God and I should make the best use of my time and the things that I'm good at and remember to thank him each day and ask him to guide me in everything I say and do. |
| Voice 1 | Right. Remember also that the people who asked Jesus the question that received that answer, were trying to trick him. Presumably, you are not. |

© *Heather Johnston*
(*Based on Matthew 22:21, Mark 12:17, Luke 20:25*)

## Cash Power

| Reader 1 | I only buy clothes with a decent label. |
|---|---|
| Reader 2 | I usually buy my clothes at Marks & Spencers or Debenhams or somewhere like that. |
| Reader 3 | I go to my local church 'New to You' and charity shops. |
| Reader 4 | Jesus said, 'Why worry about clothes? Look at how the wild flowers grow: they do not work or make clothes for themselves. But I tell you that not even King Solomon |

with all his wealth had clothes as beautiful as one of these flowers. It is God who clothes the wild grass – grass that is here today and gone tomorrow, burnt up in the oven. Won't he be all the more sure to clothe you?' (Matthew 6:28–30).

*PAUSE*

R 1     I buy pre-prepared food from Sainsbury's, if we're not going out for dinner.

R 2     I buy quite a lot of convenience food these days.

R 3     I've got an organic allotment and I'm more or less vegetarian.

R 4     Jesus said, '. . . I tell you not to be worried about the food and drink you need in order to stay alive . . . After all, isn't life worth more than food?' (Matthew 6:25).

*PAUSE*

R 1     I'm glad they give you those big wheely-bin things, I only wish we could have two, ours is always so full.

R 2     I think it's *disgusting*, the stuff they're allowed to put in the rivers and everywhere, and what you see on the beaches these days – well!

R 3     I think it's disgusting too – so I recycle glass and paper, and my food and drink cans, plastic bottles, my wellies, waste clothing and shoes, engine oil, furniture – oh, and I *always* look in skips.

R 4     Jesus said, 'Why do you look at the speck in your brother's eye but pay no attention to the log in your own eye? How can you say to your brother, "Please, brother, let me take that speck out of your eye," yet cannot even see the log in your own eye? You hypocrite!' (Luke 6:41–42a).

*PAUSE*

R 1     I give to charity when I'm asked. Doesn't everyone?

R 2     I try and give to good causes, but money's so tight these

days, isn't it? So I can't manage much. I'll give more if I
come up on the lottery!

R 3    I organize my regular giving so the tax can be reclaimed
by the recipient, and I try to be generous in what I give –
and I find it seems to come back anyway, somehow or
other, when I need it!

R 4    Jesus said, 'Do not store up riches for yourselves here on
earth, where moths and rust destroy, and robbers break
in and steal. Instead, store up riches for yourselves in
heaven, where moths and rust cannot destroy, and
robbers cannot break in and steal. For your heart will
always be where your riches are' (Matthew 6:19–21).

© *Edmonde-Mary Openshaw Gill*

## 'The harvest is large, but there are few workers to gather it in' (Matthew 9:37)

This script should be read slowly by four people, with the voice
of God coming from someone unseen (perhaps over speakers), if
possible.

*Who will gather my harvest?*
*Who will do the work?*
*Who will teach and train them?*
*Who will give the workers their due?*

I would give more of my time,
but I spend so much of it
ferrying my children around –
you know how it is.
And I don't want them to grow up
thinking
I don't put them first.
Because that's how it should be.
Isn't it?

I would give more of my expertise,
but I come home at night
and my favourite programme's on –
not that I watch much TV –
then before I know it,
it's bedtime!
And I know you'll agree
that we all need time for ourselves!
Don't we?

I would give more of my money,
but to be honest,
I'm not quite sure
how much I should put in
and all together, everyone's loose change
must mount up!
And I do need another break –
everyone's entitled to holidays!
Aren't they?

*Who will gather my harvest?*
*Who will do the work?*
*Who will teach and train them?*
*Who will give the workers their due?*
*Or will my harvest rot?*

© *Edmonde-Mary Openshaw Gill*

# 9

# Intercession

## Making Connections

All things come from God and of his own do we give. Our prayers need to be part of the constant interchange of receiving and giving which is our life in Christ.

Intercessions should be real and from the heart. What you read in this section can be used as printed, but it may be better to make it your own, using your own words and addressing your own situation.

The whole world of money concerns us all and may be very troubling. Yet we rarely hear it mentioned in public prayer. We must bring the problems, the shortages, the abundances and the difficult issues all to God.

Make sure that the intercessions are connected to the themes and content of the whole service. They are there to capture the issues and lay them before God as we seek the help of the Holy Spirit to align ourselves with his will.

Don't ignore the potential of periods of sensitive silence. Silence often speaks more loudly than words. Linking different aspects of the service through topics and leaving periods for reflection can reinforce the direction of the worship. Prayers spaced with silences give the issues time to sink in, and worshippers time to listen to what God is saying.

*Periods of silence may be kept and appropriate responses may be used.*


Loving God, giver of all that is,
we pray to you in faith with thanksgiving.
We pray for ourselves and for each other,
for our families and loved ones.
We give you thanks for all who care for us.
Give us grace to see Christ in others
and to love others as he loves us.

We rejoice in your steadfast love
offered to all through Jesus Christ.
We ask your help for all who suffer.
Bless all who seek to bring your help to them.

We praise you for all your gifts to us,
for the world and all that is in it.
Help us and all your people
to share every sort of wealth.
Teach us to act with justice
so that there may be peace.

We pray for your Church,
for all who serve Christ and his kingdom.
Strengthen us
for our work and witness in the world.
Grant us wholehearted generosity,
so we may live in liberty
and reflect your glory in the world.

We give thanks for those who have died,
for those who have gone
before us in the faith,
and those whose faith
is known to you alone.
Grant us, with them,
entry into your heavenly kingdom.

Generous and merciful God,
loving and giving God,
you look with compassion
on all who turn to you:

**accept these prayers
for the sake of your Son,
our Saviour Jesus Christ.
Amen.**

---

### Stewardship and Prayer

Stewardship is an emotive area and the intercessions can bring
about new thinking and a new sense of ownership. Meditations
and sermons need to be linked into prayer and the whole service
given a feeling of unity. If links are not put into place ideas will
lack coherence and an irritation factor can set in. It is with the use
of silence and linking sentences that the service shows the
stewardship of time as an experience, the stewardship of skills is
begun to be understood and the stewardship of wealth is given
and received.

## 10

# Gathering of the Gifts

---

**What is the Offertory?**

Ambiguities and confusions are particularly evident around the words we use at that time in worship when the gifts of the people are gathered: alms, oblations, offertory. Are alms and oblations for the Church or for the poor? Is the offertory the cash or is it the bread and wine? Perhaps the answer to these questions is: 'Both'.

---

Lord God,
by this holy exchange of gifts
you share with us your divine life.
Grant that everything we do
may be directed by the knowledge of your truth.
We ask this in the name of Jesus the Lord.

*The Roman Missal © 1973, International Committee on
English in the Liturgy, Inc. All rights reserved*


Father,
from all you give us
we present this bread and wine.
As we serve you now,
accept our offering
and sustain us with your promise of eternal life.
Grant this through Christ our Lord.

*The Roman Missal © 1973, International Committee on
English in the Liturgy, Inc. All rights reserved*

Everlasting God,
you have given us all we have,
your bounty supplies all our needs:
we, your humble servants,    *who love a serve you,*
offer you this token of our gratitude
for all your mercies.
Amen.

*© The Episcopal Church in the Philippines*

---

### Gathering the Gifts

The gifts of the people may be gathered in silence, adding solemnity and emphasis to the action, or with musical accompaniment or during a hymn. Sentences from scripture (see ch. 1) or other suitable prayers (see p. 7 above) may be used.

---

## Offertory Prayers

(*money*)
Blessed are you, Lord, God of all creation;
through your goodness we have our money to offer.
Fruit of our labours, symbol of our commitment.
It will become a tool to be used for your glory.
**Blessed be God for ever.**

(*time and skills*)
Blessed are you, Lord, God of all creation;
through your goodness we have our time and skills to offer.
Fruit of our lives and experience.
They will become tools to be used for your glory.
**Blessed be God for ever.**

*Stewardship Network Resource Book*

We give what we have, but not all –
    help us to be more generous.
We serve as we are called –
    help us to see when you are calling us further.
We love within our limits –
    help us to break down those barriers.
So that we may love and serve you and give wholeheartedly.
In Jesus' name.

© *Marjorie Dobson*
*First appeared in* Open with God, *published by the West Yorkshire Synod of
the Methodist Church, District Office, 19 Wentworth Court, Rastrick,
Brighouse, West Yorkshire,* HD6 3XD

We hand you our gifts on a plate,
you gave us your life on a cross.

Help us to reconcile the difference
between our giving and yours,
for Jesus' and the world's sake.

© *Marjorie Dobson*
*First appeared in* Open with God, *published by the West Yorkshire Synod of
the Methodist Church, District Office, 19 Wentworth Court, Rastrick,
Brighouse, West Yorkshire,* HD6 3XD

Blessed are you, Lord, God of all creation;
through your goodness we have these gifts to share.
Accept and use our offerings for your glory
and for the service of your kingdom.
**Blessed be God for ever.**

*Source unknown*

Blessed are you, Lord, God of all creation;
the source of all life and giver of all good things.
We offer you this proportion of the wealth
you have enabled us to create and enjoy,
in token that all things are yours.
**Blessed be God for ever.**

*D. A. Hunter Johnson (adapted)*

### *All Things Come From You*

In our communion rites the rubrics have often tended to suggest
that the following prayer is used as the offerings of the people are
collected and presented:

'Yours, Lord, is the greatness, the power, the glory, the splendour,
and the majesty; for everything in heaven and on earth is yours.
All things come from you, and of your own do we give you.'

The intention has been to keep the money offering separate from
the placing of the bread and wine on the holy table. But popular
usage has merged the two. This should not surprise or disappoint
us – we often think of the bread and wine as representing all
that God gives us, and it is also right and proper to think of our
money offerings as representative of the whole of our lives and
endeavours.

   Perhaps there is an important insight in this common usage,
which has a lesson for liturgical purists. There is an opportunity
here for our worship simultaneously to operate on different levels:
providing the enrichment of overlapping layers of meaning. Why
are we too squeamish to accept this added significance for people
who live in an economic rather than an agrarian culture? Here we
offer threefold offertory prayers that acknowledge and clarify
these layers of meaning.

*Accepting the alms,*
Blessed are you, Lord, God of all creation;
through your goodness we have this money to offer,
the fruit of our labour and of the skills you have given us.
Take us and our possessions to do your work in the world.
**Blessed be God for ever.**

*Taking the bread,*
Blessed are you, Lord, God of all creation;
through your goodness we have this bread to offer,
which earth has given and human hands have made.
For us it becomes the bread of life.
**Blessed be God for ever.**

*Taking the wine,*
Blessed are you, Lord, God of all creation;
through your goodness we have this wine to offer,
fruit of the vine and work of human hands.
For us it becomes the cup of salvation.
**Blessed be God for ever.**

*Liturgy 1975*
© *Church of the Province of Southern Africa*

O Lord our God,
maker of all things.
Through your goodness you have blessed us with these gifts.
With them we offer ourselves to your service
and dedicate our lives
to the care and redemption of all that you have made,
for the sake of him who gave himself for us,
Jesus Christ our Lord.

*Reprinted from Lutheran Book of Worship, © 1978, by permission of*
*Augsburg Fortress*

Leader　　Let us now bring our offerings to God as signs of our self-giving, praying for God's Spirit to transform us and our gifts.

*(The gifts of the people are gathered and brought up to the altar with the bread and wine for the Eucharist and other examples of God's goodness as appropriate for the season. Music may be played or songs sung.)*

Leader　　Glory to God, source of all bounty and beauty whose fullness and fragrance can transform us within and without.

People　　Creator God, we lift our hearts to you in thanks.

Leader　　Glory to God, who has made a covenant with all living creatures and has promised never to forsake the creation he loves.

People　　Creator God, we lift our hearts to you in thanks.

Leader　　Glory to God, who made us all in his image, and entrusted earth and her life to our care.

People　　Creator God, we lift our hearts to you in thanks.

Leader　　O God, Redeemer of all things, with grateful thanks we offer these gifts and this bread and wine, fruits of your earth and of our labour, and signs of your redemptive purpose for our lives and for all creation. By sharing in this bread and wine you assure us, in Christ, of a share in your being, your bliss, your purpose.

People　　Glory to God, our Redeemer, who saves us by his grace.

*Extract adapted from Liturgy of Church of South India*

*Exchange of Gifts*

At the heart of Christian worship, the Eucharist celebrates an extraordinary exchange of gifts. We can give God nothing. This is a truism, but somehow I am allowed to fly in the face of it. Outrageously I find my own offering mysteriously intertwined with the offering of Jesus: I find myself being of the Body of Christ.

We bring our offerings of bread and wine to represent the offering of our whole lives. My giving of money, gathered at the same time, also aspires to do this. It may do it unworthily, but this is part of my journey in the way of Christ. My giving does not separate off a part of my money for sanctity – it aspires to represent the whole and bring the whole before God, to become sacramental, an outward and visible sign for me and mine. It is a symbol of where I am on my journey, a personal representation in parallel with the communal representation of the Eucharistic elements.

Worship derives from *worth-ship*, a peculiarly English formation. In worship I proclaim God's worth. If I risk making what I give in money part of that proclamation, interweaving it with word and sacrament, I become open to deeper and deeper questions about my life before God. So the Body of Christ, and I as part of that Body, can aspire to represent the givingness of God to the world.

# II

# Prefaces

You ask us to express our thanks by self-denial.
We are to master our failings and conquer our pride.
We are to show to those in need your goodness to us.

All things are of your making,
all times and seasons obey your laws,
but you chose to create humanity in your own image,
giving us the care of the whole world in all its wonder.
You made us stewards of creation,
to praise you day by day for the marvels of your wisdom and power.

**Responsive Preface**

Living God, we give you thanks and praise that you protect us by
    your power;

Through your mercy
**We rejoice in a living hope.**

In Christ our Saviour you have brought us to new birth;

Through your mercy
**We rejoice in a living hope.**

By the rising of Jesus Christ from the dead
You bring us to new life, which nothing can destroy;

Through your mercy
**We rejoice in a living hope.**

By trust and faith in you we receive the joy of salvation;

Through your mercy
**We rejoice in a living hope.**

We are filled with wonder, glory and joy, praising you and saying:
**Holy, holy, holy Lord . . .**

*Stewardship Network Resource Book (adapted)*

You have no need of our praise,
yet our desire to thank you is a gift from you.
Our prayer of thanksgiving adds nothing to your greatness,
but makes us grow in your grace.

*The Roman Missal*
© *1973, International Committee on English in the Liturgy, Inc.*
*All rights reserved*

**Responsive Preface**

Father, you give and we receive,
**Help us, in love, to share.**

Thank you for life, for all we are and all we have;

Father, you give and we receive,
**Help us, in love, to share.**

Thank you for the beauty and goodness around us;

Father, you give and we receive,
**Help us, in love, to share.**

Thank you that we are special to you, and you need us;

Father, you give and we receive,
**Help us, in love, to share.**

Thank you that you trust us with gifts, which tell of your love;

Father, you give and we receive,
**Help us, in love, to share.**

We are filled with wonder, glory and joy,
praising you and saying:
**Holy, holy, holy Lord . . .**

*Stewardship Network Resource Book*

# Thanksgiving after Communion

Dear Father God, your love is constant.
We rejoice in the gift of your Son,
who became poor that we might become rich.
Thank you for giving us the rich food
of his body and blood.
By your Spirit enable us to respond cheerfully,
by giving ourselves generously to you and to others,
all our days.
Through Jesus Christ our Lord.

*Stewardship Network Resource Book*

Lord, you have created and redeemed us.
Grant that our faith may bear the abundant fruit of justice and
   charity,
So that all may see our good works and glorify your name.
Through Jesus Christ, our Lord.

*Libreria Editrice Vaticana*
*00120 Città del Vaticano*

Here at your table,
loving and righteous God,
we know your boundless generosity exceeds
   all that we can desire or deserve:
liberate us from all jealousy and greed,
that we may be free to love and serve others,
and in your service may find our true reward;
through Jesus Christ our Lord.

*Prayer Book for Australia (adapted)*

Gracious God,
you have given us much today;
grant us also a thankful spirit.
Into your hands we commend ourselves
and those we love.
Remain with us, strengthen us,
and renew us for the service of your Son Jesus Christ.

*A New Zealand Prayer Book (adapted)*
*Anglican Church in Aotearoa, New Zealand and Polynesia*


Fill our hearts with faith, Lord God,
until they overflow in loving care;
that the hungry may be fed,
the homeless housed,
and every hurt be healed:
through the compassion of Jesus Christ our Lord.

*© Michael Counsell*
*Prayers for Sundays*
*(HarperCollins Publishers Ltd 1994)*


Giving Father,
We receive so much from you,
and therefore have much to give.
Help us to discover, develop, and direct our gifts
that we may be lively agents of your love.

*Stewardship Network Resource Book*


O God, to our stewardship you have entrusted the vast resources of
    creation.
May there be no lack of bread at the tables of any of your children;
but stir up within us as well a longing for your word,
that we may be able to satisfy that hunger for truth
which you have placed within every human heart.
This we ask through Jesus the Lord.

*Libreria Editrice Vaticana*
*00120 Città del Vaticano*

Giver of life and love,
we thank you that in this heavenly banquet
you invigorate and renew us.
Living in the unity of the Spirit
may we boldly use your gifts
to continue your work in the world.

*Prayer Book for Australia*

# 13

# Blessing

May God who loves a cheerful giver,
and gives us all things in Christ,
swell the harvest of your benevolence.
**Amen.**

May Christ who for our sake became poor
make you rich in everything –
in faith, speech, knowledge and love.
**Amen.**

May the Holy Spirit who gives gifts to all people,
flood your hearts with thanksgiving to God.
**Amen.**

And the blessing of God Almighty,
the Father, the Son, and the Holy Spirit,
be among you and remain with you always.
**Amen.**

*Stewardship Network Resource Book*

# 14

# Hymns and Songs

All-creating heavenly giver,
bringing light and life to birth;
all-sustaining heavenly Father
of the families of earth:
We, your children, lift our voices
singing gladly of your love:
never-ending are the praises
rising to your throne above.

Ever-living Lord and Saviour,
breaking chains of sin and shame;
ever-loving intercessor,
prayers are answered in your name:
We, your servants, liberated
at a fearful ransom-price,
in your kingdom are united
by that mighty sacrifice.

Life-conceiving wind of heaven,
breathing gifts upon us all;
life-enhancing Spirit, given
to enrich us, great and small:
We, whose talents widely differ,
now restore to you your own,
and in true thanksgiving offer
all we are before the throne.

Father, Son and Holy Spirit,
blessing all within your hand:
full the cup that we inherit,
firm the ground on which we stand:
We, your people, undeserving
of the grace you freely give,
now and ever, in thanksgiving
to your praise and glory live.

*Words © Michael Saward/Jubilate Hymns*
*87 87D*
*Mead House*
*Lux Eoi*
*Everton*

All you have given calls us, Lord, to praise you –
Abundant wealth through Jesus Christ our Lord –
Your peace to guard our hearts in times of trouble;
Our needs supplied, our broken strength restored.

Teach us to use your varied gifts with wisdom,
Sharing with others for the good of all;
May we delight in giving and receiving,
And hold each other up, that none may fall.

To you, our God and Father, be the glory,
For in all things the praise belongs to you;
We pledge our thankful service to your people,
That we may show your love through what we do.

*© Jenny Dann*
*(Based on Philippians 4:4–20 and 1 Peter 4:7–11)*
*11 10 11 10*
*Strength and stay*
*Highwood*

And did you risk yourself, O Christ,
for such a world as ours,
into its hands to yield your life,
your name, your gifts and powers?

So few had seen and touched and heard,
so few received your love! –
but now your Spirit and your word
have sent us on the move.

What stories fill those early days
of saints whose names we know,
who risked their lives to speak your praise
and saw your kingdom grow!
    What news escapes to reach us now
    and shames our little faith! –
    believers risking all for you
    through prison, pain and death.

Lord, help us to release our grasp
on all that chokes the seed,
on all that undermines our task
or contradicts our creed;
    to find the new security
    of launching into space
    when you baptize us, set us free
    and give the opening grace!

No status, goods or power of choice,
no right and no renown
can matter when we hear your voice
and glimpse your thorny crown:
    when we are least in human eyes
    in you we are most strong;
    can this be risk, to die, to rise
    with you, our Glory song?

*Words: © Christopher Idle/Jubilate Hymns*
*(Based on Acts 15:26. Written for the Baptist Union Assembly 1997)*
*D C M*
*Kingsfold*
*Forest Green*

## Giving

A rich young man came seeking
The final steps to heaven,
For he had been obedient
To each commandment given.
But Jesus asked the courage
To give his wealth away.
The young man turned in sorrow,
That price he could not pay.

The rich men's gifts were lavish
And made for public show.
The widow's gift was humble
And only God would know.
In giving to the Temple,
Although her coins were small,
Her gift had so much meaning
Because she gave her all.

One boy brought loaves and fishes.
No other food was there.
But Jesus fed the thousands
And still had bread to spare.
That miracle of plenty
Soon spread beyond that place,
The simple gift he offered
God multiplied by grace.

Lord, keep our love of money
From turning into greed.
Help us to use it wisely
To meet each other's need.

For whether poor or wealthy,
We have so much to share
And open-hearted giving
Will show your loving care.

Body broken for our good,
and that body's precious blood:
we receive them to our shame,
who dishonour Jesus' name.
Every day more blood is shed;
flesh is broken, left for dead.
Where earth's children bleed and die,
it is Christ we crucify.

Yet your love, God, draws us near,
though unworthy to be here;
we have nothing good to bring,
yet you give us everything.
Here you give us Christ who died,
resurrected, glorified;
his humanity, divine,
here is ours in bread and wine.

In communion with the Lord,
faith, hope, love are all restored;
here is wealth beyond compare,
wealth for all the world to share.
He reclaims our every breath:
all our life and even death
cannot be too great a price,
to fulfil his sacrifice.

Time, with energy and health,
talent, poverty or wealth:

all are yours, Lord, taken up
in the sign of bread and cup.
Though we may be broken too,
and our lives poured out for you,
make of us the living sign
of your love in bread and wine.

*Alan Gaunt © 1999 Stainer & Bell Ltd*
*77 77*D
*Salzburg (Hintze)*
*Aberystwyth*

## All Splendour and All Majesty

Eternal God, we bring our praise
to you, our Father and our Friend;
to you, whose word has never failed,
    whose reign shall never end:

all greatness and all power are yours,
all splendour and all majesty –
for over heaven and earth you rule
    with total sovereignty.

Your kingdom stands for evermore –
enthroned on high, you are the King!
Let every tongue acknowledge you
    as Lord of everything.

Our wealth and honour come from you;
from you are strength and power and fame;
how glad we are to give you thanks
    and magnify your name.

But who are we to worship you,
to make our offerings at your throne?
Whatever gifts we choose to bring
    have come from you alone.

Let all that we possess be yours –
ourselves, our lives, our riches too;
confessing you as Lord and God
we bow and honour you!

## Give Thanks

Tune: BURGESS HILL

Words: Martin Leckebusch     © by Ian Sharp

- na - tion, *give thanks to the Lord;* for

love which tru - ly frees us to know the One who

sees us i - den - ti - fied with Je - sus *give*

thanks,　　　give　thanks　　to　　the　Lord!

For riches of salvation
   give thanks to the Lord;
release from condemnation,
   give thanks to the Lord;
for love which truly frees us
to know the One who sees us
identified with Jesus –
   give thanks, give thanks to the Lord!

For courage and endurance
   give thanks to the Lord;
the Spirit's reassurance,
   give thanks to the Lord;
for fatherly correction,
the call to share perfection,
the hope of resurrection –
   give thanks, give thanks to the Lord!

For life in all its fullness
   give thanks to the Lord;
for all that leads to wholeness
   give thanks to the Lord

who knows our every feeling
and speaks in grace, revealing
encouragement and healing –
   give thanks, give thanks to the Lord!

For justice with compassion
   give thanks to the Lord,
and freedom from oppression
   give thanks to the Lord;
for holiness unending,
a kingdom still extending,
all earthly power transcending –
   give thanks, give thanks to the Lord!

*Martin Leckebusch*
© *Kevin Mayhew Ltd, Buxhall, Stowmarket, Suffolk IP14 3BW*
*Used by permission*
*Can be used as a litany*

God is the giver of all things that are;
worlds without end were fashioned by his hand,
from earth's foundations to the furthest star,
in splendour shining, countless as the sand.

God is the giver: from his love derive
each conscious being, all our life and breath,
by whose sustaining care we live and thrive,
our strong deliverer at the gates of death.

God is the giver, always, everywhere,
through every harvest that the world affords;
so may we learn the gifts of God to share:
we are but stewards, earth is still the Lord's.

God is the giver, for he gave his Son
to bear with us our nature and our pain,
who on the cross our forfeit freedom won,
who from the grave to glory rose again.

God is the giver: he it is who showers
such gifts upon us, worthy of a King.
All things through Christ in life and death are ours;
have we no gifts of thankfulness to bring?

O God the giver, in your hands we place
our wealth, our time, and all we call our own.
Take now our love, transform us by your grace,
for all we have and are is yours alone.

*© Timothy Dudley-Smith*
*10 10 10 10*
*Woodlands*
*Eventide*
*Anima Christi*

God of love, your pilgrim people
spoke your word in every age.
Proudly raising tower and steeple,
Christians built their heritage.
Now the heirs of that tradition
have the duty to uphold
witness to the ancient vision
in a very different world.

Where an earlier generation
built a monumental frame
which a smaller congregation
often struggles to maintain,
save us from our fear of failure;
lift our eyes that we may see
how to show our living Saviour
in our own community.

Help us understand the forces
tangled in the wealth we own,
or we may misuse resources
out of ignorance alone.

Set against a true perspective
all we plan and all we do
so that we may be effective
in our stewardship for you.

God of love, your pilgrim people
speak your word in every age.
Now in church and home and chapel
help us build a heritage,
so the heirs of our tradition
have their own means to uphold
witness to the living vision
in another future world.

God, who came in Jesus,
for humanity,
when we read your teaching,
everywhere we see
that your conversations
showed where value lay,
challenged people's thinking,
showed a different way.

As you showed Zacchaeus
how his money came
out of exploitation,
so you stirred his shame.
Come to our homes, Jesus,
in these latter days.
Where our wealth is tainted,
help us change our ways.

When the rich man asked you
how to find new life,
couldn't take your answer,
couldn't face the truth.
Question our lives, Jesus,
show us how to give.
Free us from possessions,
show us how to live.

As the many women
followed in your way,
bringing their resources
to the company,
lead us forward, Jesus,
so that we may show
practical compassion
to the world we know.

© *Janet Wootton*
*65 65D*
*Evelyns*
*King's Weston*

Greenness dancing in the earth
Brings about the world's rebirth.

*Chorus*
*This is God's vitality,*
*Join the dance and set it free.*

Shared responsibility
Forms the world's ecology.

*Chorus*

Partnership within the dance
Will God's turning shapes enhance.

*Chorus*

Through God's generosity
Nature gives abundantly.

*Chorus*

Giving ourselves prayerfully
Shapes celestial energy.

*Chorus*

Bringing our gifts joyfully
Shares God's creativity.

*Chorus*

*© June Boyce-Tillman*
*77 77*
*Monkland*
*Boyce*


**To You Alone**

How privileged we are,
that we are called to bring
our offerings and gifts to you,
our Sovereign Lord and King!

It humbles us to see
the riches you provide:
to everyone who seeks your help
your hand is open wide.

What joys you pour on those
who give with pure delight –
for all who share with cheerful hearts
are precious in your sight.

Lord, as we bring our gifts
this longing we express:
that we may serve you faithfully
with all that we possess.

Within this broken world
so many needs arise;
Lord, may our use of wealth become
creative, bold and wise.

So may we worship you
with everything we own,
for all we have and give and are
belong to you alone.

*Martin Leckebusch*
*© Kevin Mayhew Ltd, Buxhall, Stowmarket, Suffolk IP14 3BW*
*Used by permission*
*SM*
*Franconia*

## Living Sacrifice

How rich and deep God's judgements are,
   his knowledge, how profound!
Who understands the path he takes?
   His wisdom, who can sound?
If we should try to guide his thoughts
   no counsel could we find
to offer the all-seeing One
   who forms both heart and mind.

And who can give him anything
   which he must then repay,
or charge a debt to his account
   against the judgement day?

Eternal glory and renown
   shall evermore be his –
the Source of all created things,
   the End of all that is!

And yet our living sacrifice
   this awesome God desires:
our mortal bodies, yielded up,
   to serve as he requires!
Such giving is a sacred act,
   such worship, pure and right:
the best response of thankful hearts,
   and pleasing in his sight.

Then by his all-surpassing power
   our minds he will transform
to see this world's ungodly ways
   no longer as the norm:
for hearts and lives renewed by grace
   at last can truly learn
God's good and pleasing will to prove,
   his judgements to discern.

*Martin Leckebusch*
*© Kevin Mayhew Ltd, Buxhall, Stowmarket, Suffolk IP14 3BW*
*Used by permission*
*(Based on Romans 11:33–12:2)*
*DCM*
*Kingsfold*
*Forest Green*
*Noël*

If this is not our world
with all its hollow powers,
to make a god of gold
is no concern of ours.
   The latest gains
   fill all the news;
   we need not choose
   to wear such chains.

If goods are not our goal
and all our wealth will rust,
I dare not lose my soul
by scrabbling for the dust.
   Not heaven nor earth
   are up for sale;
   coins are no scale
   of human worth.

If we are not our own
but purchased at a price,
to follow Christ alone
is no great sacrifice.
   In him, if we
   hold nothing back,
   we have no lack;
   he sets us free.

If Christ is all our praise,
our heritage, our health,
we need not waste our days
in struggling after wealth.
   And those who give
   their all, and more,
   will not be poor
   but start to live.

*Words: © Christopher Idle/Jubilate Hymns*
*66 66 44 44*
*Love Unknown*
*Darwall's 148th*

**All For You**

Words and Music: Ruth Thomas

I give my life to you
Nothing less will do
I give my life to you
I give my life to you.

I give my Wealth to you
Nothing less will do
I give my Wealth to you
I give my Wealth to you.

I give my Love to you
Nothing less will do
I give my Love to you
I give my Love to you.

© *Ruth Thomas*

*While these are written as two hymns, the themes are linked and they may be sung consecutively.*

## Peace For Me

Words and Music: Ruth Thomas

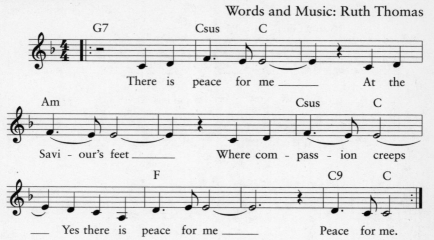

There is peace for me
At the Saviour's feet
Where compassion creeps
Yes there is peace for me
Peace for me.

There is Hope for me
At the Saviour's feet
Where my tears can seep
Yes there is Hope for me
Hope for me.

There is Love for me
At the Saviour's feet
Where I sweetly sleep
Yes there is Love for me
Love for me.

## Your promises, a gift to me

Words: Lois Ainger

Music: John Bailey

Gently and quietly ♩ = 84

(vs. 5-8)

I know my need of you you

place me where you are I feel the pain of

vs. 1-7

loss and you love and com - fort me.

v. 8    *a little faster*

So you live your life in me as I live my life in you. I live my life in you as you live your life in me.

1. I know my need of you : you place me where you are
   I feel the pain of loss : and you love and comfort me.

2. I gently turn to you : you give me all there is
   I long to put things right : and you validate my care.

3. I aim to heal past wrongs : you show forgiving grace
   I let my soul be seen : and you turn your face to me.

4. I work at making peace     :     you name me as your own
   I'm blamed when I do right :     and you hold your stake in me.

5. You place me where you are  :     as I know my need of you.
   You love and comfort me     :     as I feel the pain of loss.

6. You give me all there is     :     as I gently turn to you.
   You validate my care         :     as I long to put things right.

7. You show forgiving grace     :     as I aim to heal past wrongs.
   You turn your face to me      :     as I let my soul be seen.

8. You name me as your own      :     as I work at making peace.
   You hold your stake in me     :     as I'm blamed when I do right.

9. So
   You live your life in me      :     as I live my life in you.
   I live my life in you         :     as you live your life in me.

*© Lois Ainger*
*(Based on Matthew 5:3–11)*
*Can be sung as a psalm*

## Simplicity

Jesus lived a simple life-style,
Leaving home and friends behind.
Teaching, preaching, calling people –
Never knowing what he'd find.

Reaching out to all and sundry –
Beggar, blind man, leper, cheat.
Helping, healing, sharing, caring,
Each one's need was his to meet.

On his feet were worn-out sandals.
On his back a dusty robe.
Little money, no possessions –
Yet his message spanned the globe.

Now our world is still so selfish,
Our possessions mean so much.
Yet the poor are always with us
And they need God's loving touch.

Jesus, we would ask forgiveness,
We're so full of self-concern.
We should act with your compassion,
This world's values overturn.

Jesus, help us set our standards
By the guidance that you give,
So that we can find true purpose
In the way we daily live.

*© Marjorie Dobson*
*87 87*
*All for Jesus*

Jesus, most generous Lord,
whose nature is to give,
direct your searching word
upon the way we live.
  The hungry cry
  with none to heal;
  so make us feel
  their agony.

Once rich, becoming poor,
you filled us by your grace;
move us to care much more
about your starving race:

by love may we
bring hope to birth
and learn on earth
simplicity.

You fasted forty days
fed thousands in their need;
so touch our meals with praise
and set us free from greed.
  You travelled light
  on roads of dust,
  and pilgrims must
  keep you in sight.

No palace for your home,
no gracious dwelling there;
let us in every room
show you are welcome here.
  To death you came
  in nakedness;
  the way we dress
  is costlier shame.

Help us serve you alone –
to follow where you lead,
renouncing gods of stone
and wealth and power and speed;
  to share abroad
  your rich supplies,
  most humble, wise,
  and generous Lord.

*Words: © Christopher Idle/Jubilate Hymns*
*66 66 44 44*
*Love Unknown*
*(2 Cor 8:9)*

## This Grace of Sharing

Long ago you taught your people:
'Part of what you reap is mine –
from your cattle, bring the firstborn;
tithe the crops of field and vine.'
Though beneath the law's restrictions
we are not compelled to live,
as we reap our monthly harvest,
make us eager, Lord, to give.

What a way of life you showed us
through the Son you gladly gave:
never snared by earthly treasure,
buried in a borrowed grave –
yet to all he freely offered
riches of the deepest kind:
let us live with his example
firmly fixed in heart and mind.

In the life-style of the Spirit
giving has a central part;
teach us, Lord, this grace of sharing
with a cheerful, loving heart –
not a tiresome obligation,
not a barren legal due,
but an overflow of worship:
all we have belongs to you!

*Martin Leckebusch*
© *Kevin Mayhew Ltd, Buxhall, Stowmarket, Suffolk* IP14 3BW
*Used by permission*
*87 87D*
*Ode to Joy*

Lord, in everything I do
Let me always follow you;
Let the moments of my days
Overflow with endless praise;

Take my hands and let them move
At the impulse of your love;
Every move that I shall make
Lord, direct the steps I take.

Lord, with all your people here
You invite me to draw near;
Lord, accept the gifts I bring,
Lord, accept the praise I sing.

Take my lips and let them speak
Of your goodness through the week;
Let me echo this refrain
Till I come to you again.

As I listen to your call,
Lord, I want to give my all;
Take my heart and mind and use
All my strength as you shall choose;

All I have has come from you
And I offer back to you
Only what was yours before:
Take my life for evermore.

*77 77*D
*Nottingham (Dedication)*
*Salzburg*

## Offering

Lord Jesus Christ, you call us here,
your guests, who share your bread and wine,
your friends, who draw their strength from you
as branches from the fruitful vine.

All we possess is held in trust;
from this, your bounty, we can bring
these gifts to show our thanks to you
for life, and faith, and everything.

In giving may we know the joy
which all those generous hearts possess
who know and trust your love for them,
and revel in your faithfulness.

We cannot boast of what we give,
nor ever speak of sacrifice;
for, standing at your cross, we see
that you have bought us at a price.

Who knows what wonders you have planned?
Who fathoms what your power can do?
Lord, may your love so rule our lives
that we in all things honour you.

© *Basil Bridge*
*L M*
*Solothurn*

Lord, show us how to live
set free from waste or greed,
content with what you give,
concerned for all in need.

Our choking seas and soil,
our fields diseased and sore –
what we so quickly spoil
you only can restore.

But we were brought to birth
creation to subdue,
to tend your teeming earth,
co-workers, Lord, with you.

By learning how to share,
your faithfulness we prove;
by discipline and care
our lives reflect your love.

O Father, come to heal
where your good gifts decay;
O Spirit, give us zeal,
O Saviour, show the way!

Our shame is to destroy
or leave your work undone;
our duty and our joy
to make your goodness known.

*Words: © Christopher Idle/Jubilate Hymns*
*(Based on James 5:1–6)*
*66 66 (Iambic)*
*St Cecilia*

## Dedication

Lord, you call us to your service,
Each in our own way.
Some to caring, loving, healing;
Some to preach, or pray;
Some to work with quiet learning,
Truth discerning,
Day by day.

Life for us is always changing
As your work we share.
Christian love adds new dimensions
To the way we care.
For we know that you could lead us,
As you need us,
Anywhere.

Seeing life from your perspective
Makes your challenge plain,
As your heart is grieving over
Those who live in pain.
Teach us how, by our compassion,
We may fashion
Hope again.

Lord, we set our human limits
On the work we do.
Send us your directing spirit,
Pour your power through,
That we may be free in living
And in giving
All for you.

*Marjorie Dobson*
© *LPMAA*
*Local Preachers Mutual Aid Association*
*This hymn was first published in Faith in the Future, a book of hymns*
*celebrating the 150th Anniversary of the Methodist Local Preachers Mutual Aid*
*Association, 89 High Street, Rickmansworth, Herts,* WD3 1EF
*85 85 843*
*Angel Voices*

Lord, You can't help overflowing
Into all things, near and far;
Love, eternally outgoing,
Is what makes You what You are.

In our music, in our verses,
We are quick to praise Your name;
May our bank accounts and purses
Be as quick to do the same.

Be Yourself our motivation;
Be the reason why we give;
Let your shared imagination
Shape the style in which we live.

In our being, in our doing
By Your grace we'll work with You,
in self-giving self-renewing
Easter people, through and through.

*© Elizabeth Cosnett*
*87 87*
*Cross of Jesus*
*Stuttgart*

## Here is the News

Words: Cecily Taylor                    Music: 'Watendlath' by Hilary Baily

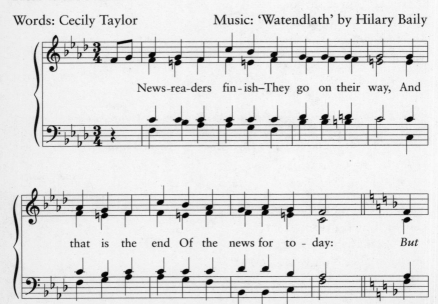

News-rea-ders fin-ish–They go on their way, And

that is the end Of the news for to-day:        But

here is the News: God's Spi - rit is li - ving Where-

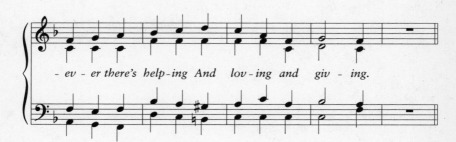

- ev - er there's help-ing And lov-ing and giv - ing.

1. Newsreaders finish –
   They go on their way,
   And that is the end
   Of the news for today:
   *But here is the News:*
   *God's Spirit is living*
   *Wherever there's helping*
   *And loving and giving.*

2. There in our illness
   Through love's tender care;
   Where comfort is given
   And sorrow is shared:
   *For here is the News . . .*

3. There in the darkness
   Where some cannot cope,
   In listening, restoring
   And giving new hope:
   *For here is the News . . .*

4. There in the famine
   Where people are fed,
   In help that is given
   To banish their dread:
   *For here is the News . . .*

5. There at the meetings
   Where nations can build
   A world made of friendship
   Where all will be filled:
   *Yes, here is the News . . .*

*Cecily Taylor*
© *1999 Stainer & Bell Ltd*

O God the Giver, you pour from your treasure
Gifts that enable your people to grow;
Fruit of the Spirit that no one can measure
Nourishes faith and provides seeds to sow.

As we receive all the riches you're giving
Teach us to use them to grow in your way:
Gifts not for hoarding, but sharing in living –
Dance to your music and join in your play.

*© Adrienne Dones/Peter Birdsey*
*11 10 11 10*
*Epiphany*

## Eucharist

O Lord God your many blessings
Fill our hearts with thanks and praise:
May this earth with all its wonders
And the moments of our days
Be used wisely for your glory
And to meet our neighbour's need;
Lord, so generous in giving,
Save us all from selfish greed.

Lord, we thank you for forgiveness,
All you give us through your Son;
May we learn to be forgiving
And to pray 'Your will be done.'
Lord, inspire us with your Spirit
As we listen to your Word;
Keep us open to fresh vision
Of your will for all the world.

Bearing one another's burdens,
Lord, we gladly intercede
For our sisters and our brothers,
Those in any kind of need;
May our giving and receiving
Teach us how our love may grow,
Till in serving one another
Heav'nly joy we come to know.

Hands outstretched receive communion.
May your grace our lives renew;
We would offer our commitment,
All we think or say or do:
Once again sent out with blessings
We would serve you evermore,
Father, Son and Holy Spirit,
Whom we worship and adore.

© *Patrick Appleford*
*87 87D*
*Lux Eoi*

## Open Our Eyes

Open our eyes to see
the anguish of the poor –
indignities untold
where life is insecure;
    then may our ears discern your call
    to demonstrate your care for all.

Open our minds to grasp
life's grim reality –
how greed and power prolong
the curse of poverty;
    and fill our mouths with words to speak,
    defending those who voice is weak.

Open our hands to give,
to serve through all our deeds,
and let our strength be spent
to meet our neighbours' needs;
    let love, not duty, be our guide:
    Lord, let our hearts be open wide!

*Martin Leckebusch*
*© Kevin Mayhew Ltd, Buxhall, Stowmarket, Suffolk IP14 3BW*
*Used by permission*
*66 66 88*
*Love Unknown*

Prodigal Father, here we stand
to give our gifts to you:
all that we have is from your hand:
your love makes our life new.

We hold as treasure from your store
the blessings of your grace:
the food and sunshine, water pure
you give the human race.

We stand indebted for all joys,
all skill, all beauty shown;
music to sing, the fun of toys
are pleasures that you loan.

We bring you money as a sign
of all we would repay:
token of what I now call 'mine';
your gift for every day.

We come as stewards of your grace,
entrusted still to show
your bounty to the human race
that all in you may grow.

We praise you for the love that dares –
in spite of all our greed –
to risk our handing on the shares
to answer human need.

*© Adrienne Dones/Peter Birdsey*
*CM*
*Gerontius*

## The Widow's Offering

Jenny Dann

Intro. Ch. *What will you give  to the*
*Lord to day___    out of _ your trea-sure store?___    Your*
*spare    ten pound notes    or your    last    twen - ty    p _____*
*which do you think is___ more?___    (Which do you think is___ more?)___*

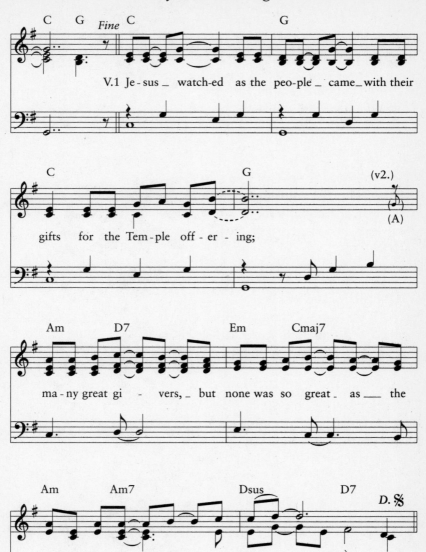

V.1 Je - sus _ watch-ed as the peo-ple _ came _ with their

gifts for the Tem-ple off-er - ing;

ma - ny great gi - vers, _ but none was so great _ as _ the

one who gave up _ ev' - ry - thing. _

*Chorus*
*What will you give to the Lord today*
*out of your treasure store?*
*Your spare ten-pound notes or your last twenty p –*
*which do you think is more?*
*(Which do you think is more?)*

*Chorus*

Jesus watched as the people came
with their gifts for the Temple offering;
many great givers, but none was so great
as the one who gave up everything.

*Chorus*

See her coming behind the rest
with two small copper coins in her hand:
a widow who had nothing else to live on
brings the costliest gift in the land.

*Chorus*

Jesus said, 'This poor widow's given
much more out of her poverty
than all the others with plenty to spare' –
now you know how God wants you to be.

*Chorus*

© *Jenny Dann*
*(Based on Mark 12:41–44)*

When love is stamped on every coin
The market and the cross shall meet,
And bulls and bears with angels join
To dance along Threadneedle Street.

But cash has meaning here and now:
It measures work and time and care;
It buys a bomb; it buys a plough;
It pays for hope; it funds despair.

Remind us always, dearest Lord,
Of what you said in Galilee:
That where we keep our treasure stored
Our hearts and minds will surely be.

So shall our dealings speak your word,
Your values keep our souls alive,
While dreams that well may be absurd
Assist creation to survive.

*© Elizabeth Cosnett*
*LM*
*Herongate*
*Winchester New*
*Angels' Lauds*

## Moratorium on Magnificat

When Mary heard her cousin say
God's promises would be fulfilled
She looked towards the coming day
And sang a song to change the world.
This is the way the world will be
When God takes on humanity.

But while the poor support the proud
And tyrants thrive in lands and homes
And while the hungry people crowd
Around the mighty on their thrones:
While greed and need go on and on
How dare we think of Mary's son?

And when it comes to you and me
To show the world a God who cares,
We duck responsibility
And hide ourselves behind our prayers.
Till we have faced our common wrong
How dare we think of Mary's song?

Now face to face with Mary's Son,
Who healed the sick and took the blame,
We'll let God's promise call us on –
And then we'll never be the same.
Then we can sing with heart and voice,
In God my spirit does rejoice.

*© Janet Wootton*
*88 88 88*
*Sussex Carol*

## Faithful Stewards

Yours the greatness, Lord, the glory,
splendour, might and majesty!
Father, Son and Holy Spirit,
ever-giving Trinity.

Generous God, we kneel astounded
that you touch our lives today
as we break this bread together,
taste the wine and pause to pray.

With our praises, Lord, we bring you
our possessions, like the lad
who entrusted loaves and fishes
to your keeping, all he had.

Take the sum of our resources:
skills and training, strength and health;
time, concern, imagination,
talents generating wealth.

Christ our Lord, transform these offerings –
Yours the resurrection power!
Ours the task as faithful stewards
to confront the present hour.

*First verse may be repeated as a final verse.*

© *Words: David Mowbray/Jubilate Hymns*
*87 87*
*Gott will's machen*
*Sussex*

## Zacchaeus was a wealthy man

Words and Music: Ruth Thomas

Zac-cha-eus was a weal-thy man, Had a
lot of mon-ey And a lot of land. Now he
heard that Je-sus was pass-ing his way.

Want-ed to see — his — face that day. So he

hid up in a sy-ca-more tree, Wait-ed for the Sav-iour

pa-tient-ly. Je-sus passed by, stopped at the — tree,

'Zac-chaeus,' he said, 'have some tea with me.' *'Come on*
*'I'll come*

*down,' he said, 'from the sy-ca-more tree, Come on*
*down,' he said, 'from the sy-ca-more tree, I'll come*

down,'_ he said,____ 'have some tea with me.    Come on
down,'_ he_ said,_ 'if you'll have tea with me.    I'll come

down,' he said, 'from the sy-ca-more tree, Come on
down,' he said, 'from the sy-ca-more tree, I'll come

Fine

down,'_ he said, 'have some tea with me.'
down,'_ he said, 'if you'll have tea with me.'    Now

stand-ing by the Lord is a mar-vel-lous thing;_

Zac-cha-eus start - ed to cry and sing._ He said, 'I'll

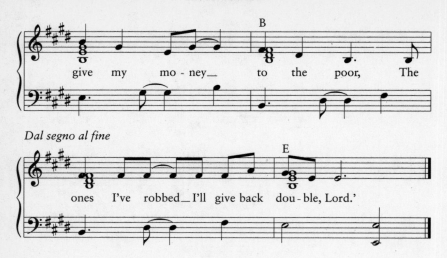

give my mo-ney__ to the poor, The

*Dal segno al fine*

ones I've robbed__ I'll give back dou-ble, Lord.'

Zacchaeus was a wealthy man,
Had a lot of money
And a lot of land.
Now he heard that Jesus was passing his way,
Wanted to see his face that day.
So he hid up in a sycamore tree,
Waited for the Saviour patiently.
Jesus passed by, stopped at the tree,
'Zacchaeus,' he said, 'have some tea with me.'
*'Come on down,' he said, 'from the sycamore tree,*
*Come on down,' he said, 'have some tea with me.*
*Come on down,' he said, 'from the sycamore tree,*
*Come on down,' he said, 'have some tea with me.'*

Now standing by the Lord is a marvellous thing;
Zacchaeus started to cry and sing.
He said, 'I'll give my money to the poor,
The ones I've robbed I'll give back double, Lord.'

'I'll come down,' he said, 'from the sycamore tree,
I'll come down,' he said, 'if you'll have tea with me.
I'll come down,' he said, 'from the sycamore tree,
I'll come down,' he said, 'if you'll have tea with me.'

*Ruth Thomas*
© *1999 Stainer & Bell Ltd*
*(Based on Luke 19:2–10)*

# 15

# Service Outlines

## Harvest

| | |
|---|---|
| Sentence | I bring the first of the fruit of the ground . . . (Deuteronomy 26:10a) |
| Penitence | When we have sown sparingly |
| Collect | Eternal God, open our eyes to see your hand at work |
| Praise | May your love be upon us, O Lord (Psalm 33) |
| Reflection | Sparse sowing, meagre reaping |
| Dialogue | The harvest is large . . . |
| Gathering of the gifts | Everlasting God, you have given us all we have |
| Preface | All things are of your making |
| Thanksgiving after Communion | O God, to our stewardship you have entrusted . . . |
| Hymns | God is the giver of all things that are |
| | Greenness dancing in the earth |
| | Lord, show us how to live |
| | O God the giver, you pour from your treasure |
| | *With traditional hymns added* |

## Christian Aid

| | |
|---|---|
| Sentence | Do not neglect to do good and share what you have . . . (Hebrews 13:16) |
| Penitence | Lord, when we have failed to recognize your presence |
| Collect | Christ Jesus, as you had compassion on the starving multitudes |
| Praise | May your love be upon us, O Lord (Psalm 33) |
| Reflection | Forgive us Lord for the crumbs of comfort |
| Dialogue | The Two-Pound Coin |
| Gathering of the gifts | We give what we have, but not all |
| Preface | You ask us to express our thanks by self-denial |
| Thanksgiving after Communion | O God, to our stewardship you have entrusted . . . |
| Hymns | All you have given calls us, Lord, to praise you |
| | And did you risk yourself, O Christ |
| | For riches of salvation |
| | God, who came in Jesus |
| | How privileged we are |
| | Long ago you taught your people |
| | Newsreaders finish |
| | Open our eyes to see |
| | When love is stamped on every coin |
| | When Mary heard her cousin say |

## Stewardship Launch

| | |
|---|---|
| Sentence | On the first day of every week . . . (1 Corinthians 16:2a) |
| Penitence | Father in creation, you are generous towards us |
| Collect | God our Father, you scrutinize our thoughts and motives |
| Praise | Glory to the Father |
| Reflection | Generous God, you ask us to trust in you for everything |
| Dialogue | How Much Should I Give? |
| Gathering of the gifts | Lord God, by this holy exchange of gifts |
| Preface | You have no need of our praise |
| Thanksgiving after Communion | Dear Father God, your love is constant |
| Hymns | All-creating heavenly giver |
| | Body broken for our good |
| | Eternal God, we bring our praise |
| | God is the giver of all things that are |
| | God of love, your pilgrim people |
| | I give my life to you/There is peace for me |
| | Lord Jesus Christ, you call us here |
| | Lord, you call us to your service |

## Stewardship Thanksgiving

| | |
|---|---|
| Sentence | Now as you excel in everything . . . (2 Corinthians 8:7) |
| Penitence | Lord, you are the fullness of grace and truth |
| Collect | Heavenly Father source of all life |

| | |
|---|---|
| Praise | May the Lord build us a house (Psalm 127) |
| Reflection | Partners of Love |
| Dialogue | 'The harvest is large . . .' |
| Gathering of the gifts | Let us now bring our offerings to God . . . |
| Responsive Preface | Father, you give and we receive |
| Thanksgiving after Communion | Fill our hearts with faith, Lord God |
| Hymns | For riches of salvation |
| | If this is not our world |
| | Lord, in everything I do |
| | Lord, You can't help overflowing |
| | O Lord God your many blessings |
| | Prodigal Father, here we stand |
| | Yours the greatness, Lord, the glory |

## Stewardship Renewal

| | |
|---|---|
| Sentence | God is able to provide you with every blessing in abundance . . . (2 Corinthians 9:8) |
| Penitence | Defender of the poor |
| Collect | Hidden God, whose wisdom compels our love |
| Praise | Hear, O my people, and I will speak (Psalm 50) |
| Reflection | Given in Love |
| Dialogue | Cash Power |
| Gathering of the gifts | We hand you our gifts on a plate |
| Preface | You have no need of our praise |
| Thanksgiving after Communion | Giving Father, We receive so much from you |

*First Fruits*

Hymns

A rich young man came seeking
God of love, your pilgrim people
God, who came in Jesus
How rich and deep God's judgements are
I know my need of you
Jesus lived a simple life-style
Jesus, most generous Lord
What will you give to the Lord today
When love is stamped on every coin

# Acknowledgements and Sources

We are very grateful to all those who have contributed new or copyright work to this book. Many items have been written especially for us and we have been greatly encouraged by the willingness of contributors and the high quality of the work they have produced. For ease of reference source details are shown beneath each item in the text, and this should be deemed to include a note of thanks in every case. Items not so identified are the work of the editors. Every effort has been made to contact copyright holders, but we take full responsibility for any errors and omissions, which should be notified to the publishers and will be rectified in any future editions.

In particular we thank the following for their support, advice and encouragement: Patrick Appleford, Barrie Gauge, David Hebblethwaite (Secretary to the Liturgical Commission), Derek Lane, Michael Saward, Martin Sellix, Christine Smith and all at Canterbury Press Norwich, Greville Thomas, Janet Wootton and the Worship Live network, members of the Church of England's stewardship network and the staff and board of the Anglican Stewardship Association.

Except where stated the scripture quotations contained herein are from The New Revised Standard Version of the Bible, Anglicized Edition, copyright © 1989, 1995 by the Division of Christian Education of the National Council of the Churches of Christ in the United States of America, and are used by permission. All rights reserved.

*Please note:* The following conditions apply where the copyright for hymns and songs is held by Stainer & Bell Ltd, Kevin Mayhew Ltd, Josef Weinberger Ltd or Jubilate Hymns. Copies may be made for local Church use if you hold a current Church Copying Licence and include the work on your return to Christian Copyright Licensing (Europe) Ltd. Alternatively, you need to write to the copyright holder for permission. The relevant addresses are:

Stainer & Bell Ltd, PO Box 110, Victoria House, 23 Gruneisen Road, London N3 1DZ.

Kevin Mayhew Ltd, Buxhall, Stowmarket, Suffolk IP14 3BW.

Josef Weinberger Ltd, 12–14 Mortimer Street, London W1N 7RD.

Jubilate Hymns, Southwick House, 4 Thorne Park Road, Chelston, Torquay TQ2 6RX.

# Index of Authors

# Index of First Lines of Hymns and Songs

# Index of Biblical References

# Subject Index